MW01289841

MASTERING THE ADVENTURE OF INTERNATIONAL DATING

A MAN'S GUIDE TO ROMANCE OVERSEAS

MARK EDWARD DAVIS

Copyright

DEDICATION

This book is dedicated to my own beauty queen, my wife Anna. Traveling the world to find you was a small price to pay for the deeply satisfying love we share.

CONTENTS

A lot has happened in 5-years.

FIFTH-YEAR IN PRINT
- UPDATED EDITION PROLOGUE -

What I wrote more than five-years ago has been proven true time and time again and blessed the many lives we've touched.

If someone would have told me that I'd be married to a former runway model from Ukraine and later be featured on a Discovery Channel documentary for creating a revolutionary new system for helping create marriages between people from different countries I would have said, "You must be mistaking me for someone else".

Back in 2004 I had a computer leasing company. My life of a salesman in California was domestic and common to most men you'd meet in America. I hadn't been outside of the US since I was a teenager in the early 1980's. But it was in 2004 that I was invited to join a group of men on a fishing trip to the Amazon River in Brazil. It was life changing in many ways, as you can imagine! Catch me in person sometime and I'll tell you the stories of Cayman hunting at night with the local natives. I was now completely fascinated with everything foreign.

A year later I traveled back to do the same fishing trip on the Amazon again, but this time we had an extended stay at the end of the trip in the city of Manaus, Brazil. The question was posed to me, "Would you like to meet some local ladies?" The man asking was a retired Navy Seal who lived there. He meant it sincerely, not to introduce me to anything seedy, but to help satisfy my curiosity for everything about this culture.

I spent that day with a wonderful young Brazilian lady. She showed me how families meet together at the beach and what life is like for Brazilians, both poor and rich. But the biggest impact she made on me was how she treated me with such value and respect. I don't remember her name, but I'll never forget the world she introduced me to.

This book will take you from that experience all the way through my first months of marriage to my Ukrainian wife Anna. But what it won't tell you is what happened in the seven years that have followed.

A few years after Anna and I married I was encouraged to write the original book, "Mastering the Adventure of International Dating", which came out in 2009. In 2010 we were on The TODAY Show with Matt Lauer, Dr. Phil Show, featured on a cable special on Women's Entertainment Network, and were interviewed on more than 50 radio talk shows. That was amazing enough, but I never could have imagined the sequence of events that would follow.

Several men who had read my book made the effort to go overseas in hopes of duplicating our success. But what they reported back to me was that they only found scammers, prostitutes and professional daters waiting for them. It frustrated me; no, it pained me deeply. I knew another side to these cultures – a warm and genuine side. I knew that my wife, her friends, and other multi-national couples we'd met were welcoming and giving people. Conversely, many of the sincere women overseas believed that many foreign men were only coming for sex vacations and they had doubts about our intentions as Westerners. The whole thing had a bad "mail order bride" stigma – and I wanted so much for good people to experience what I had experienced.

A friend named Rick said we should create our own type of retreat – a weeklong event where sincere people could meet in fun and respectful ways that could possibly lead to more multi-national marriages. We brainstormed for hours on end, day after day, about what that would look like. The result was the creation of the Quest Tour Experience, a series of introduction events we would develop and host in the country of Ukraine. Today, these tours have helped create more multi-national marriages than we could have possibly imagined when we started.

The reason for this "Fifth Year in Print Edition" is to take the book I wrote in 2009 and insert some of the wonderful things we've learned since then.

Today my wife operate Dream Connections International, Inc. along with an amazing team of brilliant and warm-hearted people: Jason, Jeff, Jerry, Juan, Lilia (my mother-in-law), Marina, Olya, Sasha, Vitali, and more. Additionally, we give back to the community there by supporting an orphanage in Anna's hometown of Nikolaev, Ukraine.

We have become thought-leaders in this world of international dating and multi-national marriage. And we've helped introduce dozens of married couples and received half a dozen proud announcements of new babies born among some of them. It's humbling to see what God has done to bless lives through Dream Connections and us.

This updated edition is for the man who is new to the idea of dating overseas – and to the man who has tried it before and only found frustration. We can tell you with assured confidence that we've really discovered something very special here – and you'll be glad you took the time to learn from what you'll find in this book. What you are holding in your hand is sound, reliable, and proven.

Grab a cup of coffee and enjoy a wonderful conversation with me in the pages that follow.

Alyona, age 30

INTRODUCTION

WHY DATE INTERNATIONALLY?

Why on Earth would anyone travel outside of their own country to date?

That's a fair question – why would you look beyond your local watering hole for romantic endeavors? Let me answer it this way. Imagine having a woman in your life who's affectionate, who completely adores you, admires you, and causes heads to turn because of her radiant beauty. Imagine having a relationship that alternates between totally comfortable and totally hot with passion. This is a woman who holds your arm as you walk down the street and looks into your eyes with such pride as if to say, "This is my man and I love him so much. He makes me feel like the luckiest woman alive." Got it?

Now, imagine this affection and adoration is coming to you from a genuine heart that has no other agenda but to make sure you are *both* happy.

Why would I describe such a scenario? Because I've been living it every day since I met Anna Astafieva in Nikolaev, Ukraine on December 10th, 2006!

So, how did it happen?

It all began when I sat down and asked myself what type of woman I wanted to have by my side and what kind of relationship I wanted to experience. That was easy. I wanted a beautiful woman with traditional values where our relationship comes first, and who loves me unconditionally (and guys, if you say that's not what you want, you're lying to yourself). Now for the hard part: where am I going to find her? In my town? Online? Local bars and clubs? Yeah, right. Or, as Dr. Phil would say, "How's that workin' for ya?"

If you live in any of the Western industrialized nations and have only dated women in your home country, then you know what the local dating scene is all about. The majority men I've spoken with describe local women in their city as being competitive, career-oriented, and internally focused on their own interests. But, for many other men – they consider looking beyond their borders because they simply feel drawn there or have met a wonderful multi-national married couple and envied the relationship they saw first hand.

For me, I discovered a new world of options by chance while traveling abroad. I can't wait for you to get to Chapter 1 so I can tell you about it! It truly caught me by surprise! But, just to be sure, I decided to fully research my discovery, as you will see. This was a life-changing revelation – I found there was another world outside of hometown. In fact, to get 'outside the box' opened me up to more options that I'd imagined possible. I was so excited with my findings I could barely contain myself as I told anyone who listen: *You've got to open your eyes to the bigger world if you want to find your ultimate match!*

Of course, the overwhelming response was less than . . . overwhelming. I've had men tell me, "Mark, I've dated Asian girls, Latinas, and Russians and they're really no different than any others."

That's when I ask them, "but were you in Asia, Russia, or Latin America when you dated them?"

"Well, no. They were here," they'd respond.

"Then that's not international dating," I'd explain. "That's not what I'm talking about."

"So what's the difference?" they'd ask. Great question. What *is* the difference?

It's bigger than you could imagine.

WHY DATE INTERNATIONALLY?

Because, thank God above, there are still some remaining cultures in this world that value what *you* bring to the table more than anything else. Yes, YOU! The secret that you don't know is that you just may be the hottest commodity on this planet to an entire world of women outside of the top "industrialized" nations. I can just hear some guy now saying, "Oh, sure, Mark. I really want to be a hot commodity to some third-world barefoot village woman!" If a guy were to actually come up to me and say something like that I'd probably fall on the floor laughing! However, that myth is part of the reason this is such a big secret – and untapped opportunity. Let me explain.

Where are the most beautiful women in the world? Sure, there are many in North America. But what do you see around your town . . . at the supermarket . . . at work?

So, where are they? They're in the countries that win the Miss Universe[1] pageant on a regular basis. In countries that I'm sure you haven't thought much about. In countries like Venezuela, Colombia, Dominican Republic, Philippines, Russia, Costa Rica, Ukraine, China, and the Czech Republic.

I'm fairly certain that these places have not been on your 'must-visit' list for dating. But that may only be true because no one took the time to tell you about them and show you a path. And do you think any of these women are poor villagers? Not a chance!

Just walk the streets, visit the markets, check out the work places of these foreign gold mines; you'll be amazed at the sheer number of beautiful women there. You won't find many overweight women, they pay attention to their style, they dress to impress, and they come from cultures that share your values. Think back to your first day in high school as a new freshman and remember how you were awestruck by nearly every girl in the hallways. Yeah, it's like that. These women have had their own challenges – and it's not economic as so many quickly jump to the conclusion. The women outnumber the men in many developing nations and then men have options: they cheat, they don't pay as much romantic attention, and the relationships don't last long. Do you value monogamy, long-term relationships, and like to be the provider in your home? You may seem too good to be true to them!

What you will learn in the chapters ahead could change your life and make you the envy of friends and strangers wherever you go.

Most men in the U.S. live lives of quiet frustration, either dating women who don't respect them or feeling trapped in relationships that are devoid of all romance. They don't know that there's an alternative. They've believed so many myths about that "mail-order-bride" thing or the "love 'em and leave 'em" stories that are actually the statistical rare exception.

International dating is a growing movement. According to the United States Congressional *International Marriage Broker's Regulation Act of 2005*[2], approximately 12,000 American men marry foreign women each year through dating tours (a number I'm confident has grown since then). These marriages are happy and experience fewer divorces by percentage than their U.S. counterparts. In fact, U.S. statistics indicate that the divorce rate among this group of men who married foreign women is around 20%[3]. Compare that with the divorce statistics in your country and you'll understand one reason international dating is growing in popularity.

Throughout this book I'll try my best to prepare you for the brave new world you're about to encounter. Your journey will be different than mine, but the sense of adventure we'll share . . . and the rush . . . and the exhilaration will be the same. I'll share with you the stories, strategies, details, and reasons why things are different around the world. I'll help you see how easy it is to travel internationally, maybe even cheaper than travel within your own country. Listen, you may be guarded, just like I was. But at some point in the next few pages ahead you'll say to yourself, "Aha, I get it!" And once the thought hits you, "I could see myself doing that", there will be a growing excitement that will build from inside when you consider how this could radically change your life forever – because you, yes *you*, could find yourself in the arms of an amazing woman from another country. You could be waking up to her *every day for the rest of your life* like so many of us do.

Let's get to it! Everything you need to make this dream a reality is in the chapters ahead.

Turn the page . . . and let's begin.

Olga, age 20

CHAPTER ONE

LOOKING FOR LOVE
IN ALL THE WRONG PLACES

Blind dates are a nightmare. I had been "set up" by a friend of mine to go out with her best friend, Angie (using her real name would be justifiably mean, but I'll refrain).

So I pull up to the address I was given and ring the doorbell. To my great delight, Angie was one of the most beautiful women I'd EVER been out with - and I mean EVER! Wow. She was 5'7" with large breasts, small waist, mid-back length brown hair and warm brown eyes. She had a slender neck and graceful posture.

I was stunned, but kept my cool. However, the entire night I was keenly aware that I was with the hottest woman I'd ever been out with – and felt a little out of my league.

Of course, I took the time to create a romantic date. I brought flowers. I'd planned dinner at an elegant restaurant on the riverfront - a window table with a view - and then a walk along the river shore after dinner.

She was funny and intriguing. She intentionally did things like ask if I was going to finish something on my plate and reach over to get it with her fork. After dinner we talked and she confessed that she did some of those things on purpose to see how I would react. She wanted to know if I was able to get past the posturing and get real. This intrigued me even further and the chemistry and sexual tension continued to build.

When I got her home we kissed in the car and then made out in her living room. I left as we were both feeling a little giddy and agreed to see each other again within the next week.

So, when does it go wrong? That sounds like a dream date? IT WAS! It was for both of us. She called her friend and told her how wonderful it went. I went home and just sent her a quick email to say that I enjoyed the evening and asked her to let me know what her schedule looked like for connecting again.

Then . . . nothing. No response. I waited until the second day to call her cell phone but only got voice mail. I called our mutual friend who told me that she wasn't sure what was up, but would find out. She called back an hour later – but wasn't sure how to tell me the news. She said that Angie called her after the date and said you guys had a great time, but she thought she was troubled that you sent her an email right when you got home. She is terrified of stalkers and you violated the 72-hour no-contact rule after a first date. WHAT!?!?!?!

Yep, that's right. I had violated her unwritten law about waiting 72.3 hours before communicating after a first date. Evidently, I learned that Angie had other "issues" in her life, but her friend hoped that we'd make a connection. She thought I was a nice guy who would help her friend find stability for her soul. Sorry, but Mr. Davis is not Dr. Phil.

Have you ever had a moment with a woman where you just step back and say, "That was really weird"? What am I saying? Of course you have! All men have! We go out into the world daring to meet and date women. We try to be ourselves just to find out that there is some unwritten code that we violated and the weirdness descends!

But that was just my first date after becoming single again. As I went out with a dozen more women – some irritating themes kept arising. I had one tell me with a condescending swagger, "I've been asked out by many men. If I went out with you, what kind of date would you take me on?" What? Is this a high school talent show and the women are hosting a panel of judges like on American Idol? I couldn't believe the in-your-face arrogance! But this was not the first or last time I would detect this type of attitude. The common theme with dating American women was, "Listen, mister, I make good money and I drive a nice car already. What else are you bringing to the table?"

Did I date some nice and sweet girls? Sure. But they didn't seem to care about their physical appearance as much and the attraction faded. Yes, Angie was just my first date after becoming single again. Yes, I was married before. But my future seemed to come down to these two questions:

Is the simple, and less expensive, life of a bachelor for me?

or

If I opted to get entangled with the fairer sex again, how can I be more successful in finding a love that makes me happy and richly fulfilled?

If you've been in a long-term relationship and considered the prospect of dating again, one of the first emotions that accompany such broken-heartedness is that of disgust and resignation. *Why would I ever want to go through that again?!?* Can I get an "amen" from the back rows? Thank you. I'm sure that there are many successful bachelors, although none come to mind at the moment. I'm sure some people prefer living alone. But that's not me - and I know it's not you either - or why would you have bought this book?

THE RESEARCH PROJECT

I spent several months in contemplation of this subject. Then, my best friend Steve Marks and I decided to make this a pragmatic research project. We ventured out to study the realm of women, relationships, masculinity, and sex. We'd read books or listen to Webinar and then reconvene to compare notes.

Most of this intellectual feasting took place over a few shots of brandy and a good cigar, as all good studies should.

In one moment of brilliance, Steve had an idea about how to make the study more scientific - taking it to the lab. I was to go on 15 dates with 15 different women with no other consideration except to get to the end of it so we could study the results. I wish there had been a simpler way to study the subject, but I was game.

The experiences were painful and frustrating dotted with moments of fun and spontaneity. I dated women who were both younger and older than me. We went different places. I averaged spending $225 on each date. I met them through Internet dating sites, set-ups from friends, and on the street.

At the end of it all, we still shook our heads trying to come to conclusions. Why was this so dissatisfying? We just couldn't put our finger on it.

Late one night, it happened: we had a moment of clarity. As we were sitting and discussing my latest date, Linda called. She was another great date, like Angie, that ended weird. She just wanted to call and tell me she had been thinking about me. Okay . . . so far so good. She said she was exhausted and had been walking a precinct for a friend of hers who was running for office, and then did some other stuff and was about to collapse into unconsciousness on her bed, but wanted to say 'hi' before she passed out. We chatted for a few minutes in her semi-conscious mind-set and said our good-byes.

After hanging up, I was numb. She really thought she was doing something nice, so why did I feel like crap?

Then this phrase hit me: *"I got the leftovers."* She gave her very best to everyone else and I got the leftovers. It hit me hard. That was exactly how I'd felt so many times before. I was not the first thought on her mind, just a 'left-over' thought.

I was done going on dates. I would rather be a bachelor than be "left-overs" to anyone ever again! I did not find what I was looking for.

I am not condemning Western women or men who find love at home. I personally believe *I was being directed* and motivated to be open to an alternative – one that was just around the corner.

I am sharing my path with you so you can find yours – wherever it may lead you. This is about you finding happiness and fulfillment. But, if you find yourself relating to what I just shared, I'm about to make your day – read on.

Nick married one of the Dream Connections' translators, Julia, who he met on a 2013 Quest Tour

CHAPTER TWO

RADICAL DIFFERENCES

Then it happened. Well, OK, it was less dramatic than that, but the results from this breakthrough were dramatic. I went on a guys' vacation trip to Rio de Janeiro. I'd been to Brazil before, but only for adventure fishing on the Amazon River, not for this kind of fun. There were six of us and we went for nine days of girls, sand, eating and drinking, girls, and girls. But not just any kind of girls – Brazilian girls!

The legend of the Brazilian beauty is justified: sensuous curves, full lips and soft eyes. This is feminine beauty defined. Every move is exotic poetry. And to watch one of these goddesses dance you'd think they had been trained to move that way. Just thinking about it . . . ah well.

We went to different dance clubs each night and spent a lot of time with many beautiful women. They were very different from the others I'd just been dating in the States. It was something about their culture and appreciation of men that grabbed my attention.

When I was with one of these bronze beauties, the questions were about me: my life, likes, interests, experiences. They would continually gauge my state of mind and body – was I hungry, bored, or thirsty? They wanted to know so they could respond in kind. When I was with one of these women, I was their world – even if it was for only that hour.

They wanted to know if I thought they were beautiful. I'd had American girls ask me if I thought they were beautiful, but they would ask in a way that demanded I acknowledge her power and that I was smitten by their looks. That was not the case here. It was asked in sincerity – hoping for a positive response.

The way they view beauty is unique. It is something they have to work for each day. They are mindful of how they dress, put on makeup, their style, posture, physical fitness, and presence. It is work for them and they just wanted to know that it was appreciated and noticed.

To give a sincere complement about some specific attribute will make them light up like a Christmas tree. It seemed to make their efforts to be beautiful all worthwhile. To enjoy being with these women was effortless. I never felt self-conscious. I was embraced like the man of the hour. And it truly was their pleasure; not just mine.

ONE OF THE GREATEST SECRETS IS REVEALED

I didn't fully understand this dynamic until Dani explained everything to me over dinner one night in Rio.

Dani and I met at one of the dance clubs and she fit right in with our group. We often had tables of 10 or 12 people since the six of us on this trip would usually have a date. Dani genuinely captivated me. She was 23-years old, but carried herself with warmth, grace, and self-confidence. She had already earned a degree in marketing and had worked for McDonald's corporate branding department there in Brazil some years before. She then opened a beauty salon, sold it, and opened a grocery store in her hometown. Now she was in Rio making plans for opening the second grocery store.

We both seemed to connect, so we made plans to spend the next day together.

Dani and me at dinner that life-changing night.

Get ready. This is when I learned the great secret.

At dinner the following night she told me more of her life story and it opened my eyes as to how these women see men. She told me she had been married before and had a two-year-old daughter. One day she found out that her

31

husband had *another wife and children* in a nearby city. She found herself living on her own with a baby on the way. Her family, especially her grandmother, helped her make it.

She told me that her story was not uncommon. She said, "It is very difficult for women here to find a good man. We know that men can't stay with just one woman – that's just not possible in Brazil. But we just hope that they will be discrete and not embarrass us.

"We say that there are three kinds of men: the Good Man, the Superior Man, and the Complete Ass. Most men are in the last category. They don't want to be faithful to their wives and they don't care about their family. They provide no money for the home and the woman has to do all the work. Most times this man will come and take what money is left – so the smart woman has to hide it.

"The good man is the one who wants to be part of the family. He will bring home some of his money from his work and actually enjoys being with his wife and kids. There is a family unit and relationship. He enjoys being the man of the house and talks to others about his wife and kids with pride.

"The superior man is rare – and not always the most desirable spouse. This is the rich business owner or maybe the mayor of the city. But those men don't usually give love or attention to their women. Some women just want the rich lifestyle, and that's why we call them Superior Men. But most women in Brazil would just hope for a good man.

"Every day, when I was married, I woke up thinking about my husband. I wanted to make sure every meal was his favorite food, his house was clean, and he was happy. I would do anything for a good man and build my world around him - even now."

It took me a while to fully grasp what she was saying. A thought began to grow as I related her story to myself. It slowly dawned on me, "I am a Good Man." I like being connected to a family. I want to have a relationship where I look forward to spending time with my wife. I am proud to be the breadwinner and financial provider for my family. I am GOLDEN here!

I have been fishing in the wrong fishing hole with the wrong bait! I was trying to bring what I had to offer to a market that didn't find it valuable. I began to believe I was not very valuable. I had been trying to sell ice to Eskimos.

One of the greatest secrets is that I am one of the most valuable commodities in the world to women in most other parts of the world! The most beautiful and exotic women in the world would find deep satisfaction in waking up each morning and pouring themselves into the love of a good man. But for most of them, the love of a good man is a dream that will never come true - if she could only find one in her country.

If you are a good man who wants to be faithful to the love of a good woman, be part of her life, and be a financial provider; then you are one of the most valuable things on this planet to most every woman in the world - outside of the industrialized nations.

Are you with me? Do you see the difference? I want to help you have the same experience and open your eyes to the value that good masculinity can bring to the world – and how rich and fulfilling your life will be as a result.

THE GOLDEN MAN

I couldn't wait to get home and tell Steve about what I'd discovered. It just made sense. It resonated deeply. I had allowed women at home to define my value. Yes, I allowed that to happen, but I didn't have a good frame of reference to help define my masculine value. I was worth a lot - just not to the group I had been dating.

I cannot begin to understate the difference this understanding makes. Being a good man is gold. I'm not talking about being an arrogant or abusive man who dominates women as a power trip. I'm talking about the average man who works hard, brings home his paycheck, works on his house over the weekend, and enjoys vacationing with his significant other. He is faithful, and dedicated, yet often unappreciated.

The good man will rarely be valued in the West as he is in these cultures. As I continued my travels to Ukraine and Costa Rica and other parts of the world, I learned that this value of the "good man" was echoed again and again.

In Eastern Europe (Russia, Ukraine and the Slavic nations), the stories may vary slightly from Latin America or the Far East, but the results are the same – the good man is gold.

So, why are the men overseas the way they are? Why are they creating such a great opportunity for us? The men that have worked and lived in a socialist or emerging country can develop a deep seeded despair over their hopes for economic improvement. One man I spoke with Ukraine explained it to me this way, "You can work hard or be lazy. It doesn't matter. Why work hard when you know that you'll always make the same amount of money. What I make today is what I'll make five years, ten years, even twenty years from now." So, for many men in this part of the world, they turn to heavy drinking, chain smoking, and sleeping around to escape the monotony.

Since they don't see economic hopes to pursue with their energies, the inner drive of the man turns to conquering more women. Staying with one woman doesn't make sense to many of the younger generations there.

This is especially true when it appears that there are more women than men in these countries. I'm not saying it just seems that way – it is a statement of fact[4].

Why would so many countries have many more women in their populations than men? Some say this phenomenon is the result of years of war in these regions taking its toll on the male population. Other studies point to unsafe drinking water and other pollutants as a possible cause. Francesca Lyman writes for **MSN Health & Fitness Online**[5]. She wrote an article entitled, *"Are Boys An Endangered Species?"* In it she states that, "Half as many boys as girls are being born in some places around the world – and pollution is the prime suspect."

Whatever the cause, it is clear that women feel they have to work hard to get a man – any man. And what kinds of men do they have to choose from? Many of them are chain smokers and heavy drinkers who have no plans for marriage in their future. Many of the women who get married find themselves as the breadwinner in the home or suffer physical abuse.

Of course, there are good men in each of these countries who will make good husbands and provide for their families. But it is a difficult task for women to make their dreams come true. The ratio of single women who are looking for a marriage relationship to that of single men who are looking for marring is so far apart that it creates major imbalance in the cultures. It's a case of supply and demand where there isn't a large enough supply of marriage-minded men.

I've heard women talk about the attitudes of men they date. They say, "If I'm sick, my boyfriend will just say, 'call me when you're better' and I better not call him until I am. That's just the way it is." Another woman told me that women always have to stay beautiful or their man will just move on. And the sex is focused on pleasing the man so they can keep him.

They have a saying among women, "A woman must always be beautiful; a man only has to be better looking than a monkey." Do you think you'll ever hear those words spoken in your country?

I just tell you all of these things so you will realize the value you bring to the table. We'll bring this into better perspective when we talk about masculinity and femininity from different cultural perspectives.

SO, WHAT DOES INTERNATIONAL-DATING LOOK LIKE?

How do we get you, the Golden Man, connected with that wonderful woman who is looking for you? International Dating is your connection.

First, let's establish some definitions. When I talk about "Dating", I'm talking about the path people take to create a *relationship* with someone new. By contrast, I'm not talking about the games played at bars to see who gets who for tonight's one-night-stand.

Having clarified our purpose, then Dating is doing anything with a woman so you can get to know her better and see how your chemistry is in person. International dating is just doing that with women in other countries.

There is a type of international "vacationer" who goes overseas to do the one-night-stand type of dating in other countries; and they search for women who can be rented by the hour for sex. I'm just not in that group.

Maybe I'm just selfish . . . I want to wake up every day with someone amazing and beautiful by my side! I went overseas dating to find someone to bring along with me through all of life's adventures.

This is where I get to share with you the shortcut to *looking for love in all the RIGHT places.* So what do you need to know to get from here to her? Here are the basic questions guys ask:

- Where should I go?

- How do I get there?

- How do I meet women once I'm there?

- What do I do with them once I've met them?

Before I learned about organized romance tours, I had to figure out how to travel, find good lodging, find the hot spots where to meet women, how to stay safe, and how to keep healthy. Most of it I gleaned from other travelers who had experience and I followed their lead. But the tricks to traveling in one city may have subtle differences from other cities. That's a lot of information to try to pass along – and is that what you really want to learn? I'll show you how to participate in an organized program where all you have to do is show up, meet eligible ladies, and have the time of your life! You'll get to enjoy a first-person walkthrough in chapter 6, but, for now, just know that it's more than possible. You can meet and marry someone from nearly any place on the globe. Yes, you can do this. In this day of easy and inexpensive travel, the world is more accessible than you've really considered. Stop limiting your options. You're living in the greatest time in history for such amazing new experiences.

The adventure starts when the plane takes off!

Anastasia, age 32

CHAPTER THREE

WHAT ARE YOU REALLY LOOKING FOR IN A WOMAN?

I am going to make this direct and simple – and I need to thank Kristina. I began writing to her through an online dating site, which I do not recommend, and you'll find out why later. Her profile said she was from Nikolaev, Ukraine. In her fourth letter to me she asked a profound question. It's a question that makes all of this very simple. She asked, "What would you like a woman to do every day, to act or be, for you to feel happy?"

What would I like for a woman to do for me every day to make me feel happy? Wow. That blew me away. Have you ever had a woman ask you a question like that?

As men and professionals, we take time to visualize success in our ventures and imagine a compelling future and then plot a course to attain it. Why don't we take that approach with the most important relationship of our lives?

Well, I decided to answer the question. I could have sent back some glib generic response, but *I decided that this whole process was part of my growth and education.* It was my time to learn about myself and to finally get specific about what I really wanted so I could make it happen.

Here's what I wrote to her:

Your question made me think about what that relationship might look like in daily life. Here's the way I see my everyday life with the woman of my dreams.

Every day in my life is a little different than the one before. But one thing that is the same is waking up each day. Each day I would wake up and see my love on the pillow next to me. We look softly into each other's eyes. I gently push her hair back away from her face and touch her shoulder. She reaches over and touches my face and softly says, "Good morning, my love". I pull her to myself and hold her. We make the moment last until we absolutely have to get up. I envision starting every day this way.

On some days, we'll work together from the office in my home. We'll get my son, Christopher, off to school and then go out for breakfast at one of the local restaurants or come home and cook breakfast. Workdays are mostly about getting tasks done. I will have calls to make and emails to write. But we find fun, humor and joy in everything we do.

My wife may want to bring coffee to me and maintain our home or she may want to work in our business. She would have her choice of things she could do. The business tasks include accounting, public relations, tourism, business writing, and basic organizing. The nice part about working from home is that we can still be together even when we are working. I envision moments when I'm sitting in my chair that she comes up behind me and puts her arms around my chest and shoulders and whispers in my ear that she loves me. I stop what I am doing to give her a kiss and tell her I love her too.

We stop to have lunch on the back porch and enjoy the sun. We go for a walk to pick Christopher up from school and walk back. Christopher does his homework while we finish our tasks. We go to the gym, dance classes, or whatever we're involved in. Later we come back home to have dinner and relax together for the rest of the evening and put Christopher to bed. While watching a movie together, we snuggle in each other's arms and pause once in a while to kiss. One of our great joys is the way we love each other in bed.

On other occasions Christopher may be staying overnight at friend's house or at his grandparents. On those occasions we may travel to Las Vegas on business, or on a personal trip to San Francisco or the wine country in Napa.

As we ride in the car with the top down and the breeze blowing in our hair, she reaches out to hold my hand; then she turns and just stares at me as if to say, "This is my man. I am so proud of him and he makes me so happy."

In return, I would give her my best. I will learn what makes her feel loved and happy. This will be my woman – and I will be so proud to have her with me. We both give each other our best – our creativity will help us find new ways of showing our love in fresh and new ways – for the rest of our lives.

I'm sure that was more than you were expecting to receive as an answer to your question. But I'm glad you asked.

It has been a few years since I wrote those words to Kristina, whom I did not marry for reasons you'll learn later in the book.

But, you can probably imagine what the results have been as a result of going through this exercise. Exactly. Every day of my life with Anna has become exactly what I wrote about in that letter – down to the last detail about surprising me in my office in the middle of the day. It pays to get specific!

Can you get specific? I'm confident you can describe her physical beauty based on your personal preferences. But can you put into words the chemistry you would feel? Can you describe the dynamics of your conversations together? Can you feel her presence in your life? What is that energy like?

When you have some down time; answer her question as if it were being asked of you. I've provided some leading questions for you to complete as an exercise. This isn't homework – it's an investment you make in creating the life of your dreams.

When you do begin your quest to find your queen, you will now have a clear idea of what you are looking for. This will help you to sort through the many girls you will date and give you the confidence to pick one to pursue.

Treat the following exercise as you would any other goal-planning exercise:

1. What is your purpose for dating overseas?

2. What are the physical attributes that are attractive to you?

3. What does a day-in-the-life with her look like?

4. What does it feel like when you talk or spend time together?

5. What does she do that makes you happy?

BONUS: I've created an online fill-in-the-blank form that will help you in your process. I call this the "7 Big Questions" survey and it is an evaluation tool for dating strategies.

Go to www.DreamConnections.com/7bigquestions.

This will guide you through the thought process you need to take.

Getting specific before you go allows you to relax and let your instincts guide you to the various women who could be exactly what you are looking for. It's like an inner GPS system leading you away from some and toward others. My dad once sent me a birthday card with these words of wisdom, "Act boldly and unseen forces will come to your aid". The dynamic is similar. Unique situations will seem to happen that just bring you to her. I can't tell you how many men have talked about the unique aspects of their stories that brought them together with their women.

Most will say, "We were so close to having not met at all – it was obviously meant to be."

In my case, I met my wife Anna when she and her friend were just about to leave the event. Mike met his wife in the lobby of the hotel where he was staying in St. Petersburg. Steve met a wonderful woman in Kherson, Ukraine, but parted ways without even getting a phone number. The next day she made the effort to track him down to the hotel where she thought he may be staying and they re-connected – and are still happily married today.

Finish this exercise and be open to the magic that will follow.

WHAT IS HER DREAM?

I came across the profile of a young woman named Elena from Kherson, Ukraine. I was impressed by how well she was able to describe her vision of life with the man of her dreams.

Listen to her heart's desire as you read her translated words:

I am very goal-oriented and I know that one day I will find my love and I will never let him go. I am tired of feeling lonely! Where are you, my true eternal love? I know you are very close to me! I am your lady and I am waiting for you. I am romantic and passionate; I am affectionate and a hot lady!

I have many goals in my life and I am sure that I will have everything I pursue, but the main goal is to have a reliable man and strong family! Life with me is unforgettable. How did you live without me? I'm sure you are missing my hugs and kisses, my care and tenderness. Do you want me to be yours? I am waiting for you to start our exciting journey for love!

I know that my man will be a perfect fit for me. He will possess all the traits of a real man! He will be smart and intelligent, polite and kind person. And I will fall in love with all the more if he loves kids! I need an understanding and caring man, who will protect me and our future family from all the difficulties in this life!

In the same way that you are becoming more specific in describing your dream girl, she is out there describing her dream man. It may be destiny that the two of you meet, but you will have to be a real man. You will have to get on a plane and pursue her. Don't worry whether you are going to the right country or you miss her – as if there were only one girl who could fit your description and make you happy. There is no lack. On the contrary, there is an overflowing abundance of ladies who would fit your description. It's kind of a 'chick idea' that there is only one "soul mate" and if you miss that one, then you're destined for second best in life.

Rest assured, if you find yourself drawn to the Elena's description, there are thousands of other ladies all over the world who have the exact same dream. I just like how she described it. My personal belief is that these ladies are looking for a traditional relationship with a good strong man – and you have been looking in all of the wrong places to find this kind of woman!

Once you are finally looking for love in all of the right places, you will find abundance – not scarcity.

Yes, this dream is alive. But I also know that you still have questions and doubts. You'll need to learn what's really behind the bad stories and stereotypes. So, let's do the man-thing and hit those concerns head on.

Chris & Anna Haste met on a Quest Tour in 2013
and married in August of 2014.

CHAPTER FOUR

SCAMS, GREEN CARDS, AND MAIL-ORDER-BRIDES

"Those who lack the courage to pursue their own dreams will always find ways to discourage others from pursuing theirs."   Mark Edward Davis

After the original printing of "Mastering the Adventure of International Dating", Anna and I appeared on The TODAY Show with Matt Lauer as advocates for international relationships. The Women's Entertainment Network (WeTV) featured our family on their cable TV program "Secret Lives of Women" – the famous "Mail Order Brides" episode. We were guests on more than 40 radio talk shows. We quickly learned how media thrives on controversy – and just how much of it they *manufacture!*

When I learned that Dr. Phil was going to do a show on "Mail Order Brides" I knew this was not going to fairly represent the majority of happy multi-national marriages. Why? Because I'd seen so many bad media pieces on foreign romance and good stories don't make for good ratings.

When I got through to one of the show's producers I told them of my wife and my story and she very candidly told me, "We're not looking for happy couples. We're looking for stories of fraud, abuse, and deceit". I convinced her that there should be at least one representative for all of the good marriages and we were given the invitation to be on the show.

As predicted, the show featured abuse, fraud, and deceit with men who were a very poor representation of who we are. We got a chance to speak to Dr. Phil on the program and tell a little of our story, but it was cut from the final version. Wow. Welcome to the world of censored media bias.

No matter how much disdain I have for it, the term "Mail Order Bride" isn't going away anytime soon. It's amazing to me how no one I've ever spoken with actually believes you can "mail order" a human being; yet they cling to this label as a means of dismissing the entire notion of finding romance overseas. Pathetic.

SO, WHAT'S THE TRUTH?

As passionate as we are about defending what we believe are superior relationships, we've also learned that there is a dark side to this industry that has made its living by exploiting the deep desires and emotions of goodhearted men – and it's just wrong.

Yes, good men are being lied to and cheated out of millions of dollars every year from fraudulent international dating websites. Your gut instincts about these types of sites are usually right. The stereotype of the fat sweaty guy in the basement corresponding with Western men as if he's a petite Russian girl named Olga from a remote village actually does have its roots in fact.

The enormous contrast between sincere international marriages and this dark industry couldn't be more extreme. On the one hand, there are tens of thousands of men who marry women from other countries every year. As previously mentioned, these have proven to be more successful marriages than their domestic counterparts and the motivation for writing this book. We want to help more sincere men and women find the kind of love that my wife and I experience every day.

However, there is a dark industry that continues to prey on the hearts of sincere men who don't have enough experience to sort the good from the bad.

To that end, I'd like to take this chapter to share with you a bit about what we've learned over these past five years so you can clearly distinguish the genuine from the fraud.

SCAMS, GOLD DIGGERS, AND GREEN CARD HUNTERS

In order to get you up to speed as quickly as possible, and so we can move on with the success strategies in the book, I'm going to deliver a crash course on the inner-workings of the international dating scams. Trust me, when you finish this chapter, you'll know more than most people on the planet know about how these scams work – and certainly more than you need to know in order to avoid them and stay on course to joining the group of happy international couples.

THE ANATOMY OF A SCAM

What is a Scam? Let me offer a solid definition for us to work with:

A scam is paying someone money who takes it with no intention of delivering what they are promising or implying is the intended purpose for the money.

So why would you consider giving money to anyone while in pursuit of a foreign wife? You would if you believed that spending that money would bring you closer to the relationship you're hoping for. Perhaps you were writing to a woman overseas who convinced you that she's looking for the same kind of relationship you are, but you need to pay for the email to be translated. You pay the fee in faith hoping that the woman is real, that you are actually writing to *her*, and that the translator is accurately communicating what you wrote. Many of these letters may be legitimate, but you can easily see how many opportunities there are for fraud in this scenario. Were you just corresponding with that sweaty guy in the basement? How would you know?

OK, that makes sense. So, what costs are reasonable to expect that are NOT a scam? Look, money will be spent in pursuit of your dreams – any and all of your dreams. Spending money testing theories or possible paths to success is not a scam – even when they don't work out. We've all known people who bought rental property at the wrong time of the market and lost that investment, yet others have retired with income they made from the same strategy. If you joined a romance tour and didn't find your life-partner on the first trip, but on a subsequent trip, does that mean the first trip was a scam? Of course not! Just because money was spent and you didn't succeed doesn't mean you were scammed. That's just an investment.

Buying this book was also a wise investment in your future happiness – if I do say so myself!

I'm fairly confident that you're with me on all of this. It just makes sense. So let's talk specifically about some of the strategies that are being used to scam men today so you'll know what they look like.

DATING SCAMS

The Internet is where most frauds take place. Why? There's very little accountability. I know of one dating site that posted 2,000 profiles and made a lot of money from men corresponding with the ladies shown in the profiles. They charged nearly $10 for each letter/email that they translated in the name of the women. The problem? They didn't know any of the ladies! They copied the photos and profile information from other sites and posted them as if they were girls that they had interviewed. They had no idea who any of the real girls where or how to contact them if they had to. However, since most men never get past the letters and actually get on a plane, their bluff was rarely called. When a man would decide to come visit his foreign pen pal, she would suddenly find a reason to break it off with him or just not be available.

I wish this was a rare exception, but it's not. This fraudulent practice has become a multi-million dollar business that is promulgated by hundreds of international dating sites around the world. This was a key motivation for the formation of www.HonestDatingSites.org, an education and watchdog site dedicated to helping men avoid the landmines in their pursuit of a foreign spouse.

To round off your education on scams, here are several common dating scams. Your instincts are probably right when you suspect one of the following to be less than legit:

1. When you receive letters from foreign women that weren't initiated by you

    a. Traditional women overseas want to be pursued – for them to initiate a letter would ruin part of the attraction – but the agencies make a lot of money from men who pay to read those emails anyway!

2. When the Agency sells her contact information or email address

    a. The dating site may offer to sell her email address or contact information. It rarely works and may not even comply with privacy laws

3. When the agency charges you for IMBRA background checks

    a. Read the requirement so of the IMBRA regulation for US citizens sometime. What they are required to do is minimal and shouldn't be charged

4. When the ladies' letters are too generic and don't answer your questions

    a. Many of these agencies that write on behalf of the women are actually using pre-written templates. If your gushy letters don't answer your questions, you've found an uncreative translator who can't figure out how to insert the answer to your questions into the template response letters she's been given

5. When she falls in love with you after the first few letters

    a. This is ridiculous. The real ladies are going to be skeptical until they meet you in person

– and even then they will want to see if you keep up the interest after you've returned home. It may happen that you can exchange sincere affection in letters, but hold on to your heart until you meet face to face

6. When the letters start asking for money (internet access/sick parents, computer, phone) before you've even met

    a. Don't give any money to any woman until you've met in person and both committed to a boyfriend/girlfriend relationship. When the money requests come in, it's a red flag, but you can simply answer, "I will definitely take care of my woman when I have a committed relationship. If that became us, I'd be glad to talk about it, but not until then."

7. When you are video chatting with someone who is online 12 hours/day

    a. Ukrainian women don't have time to be on chats for long unless it's their job.

SCAMS IN PERSON OVERSEAS

I've traveled to nearly 25 different countries now and nearly always go with someone who knows the area –

preferably a local. That solves most problems people encounter when traveling abroad. Going in a group is even better.

Many men have ventured out to travel overseas and date women on their own. Rarely do these trips produce the results they were hoping for. In most cases, these men were preyed upon by the local agencies to fleece the men for what they could get. Here are the types of scams they've reported back to me in one form or another.

<u>Agency Translators</u> – The agency requires you to use the translator that works for them – so you don't know whose side she's on: yours or her agency. The typical rates are $15 to $20 per hour US. Often they will work together with the woman you're dating to run up the translator bill and split it between them – and they never had any serious romantic intentions.

<u>Taxi Drivers</u> – The translator or the date insists on using a driver she knows. Typically, this person is a friend or family member. The Western man doesn't know what to do when he's told how much to pay the taxi driver (sometimes up to $100), so he just pays it.

<u>Restaurants</u> – The translator and the date insist on going to a favorite restaurant and you have no way of knowing if you are being overcharged. Sometimes they work out a deal with the restaurant owner in advance to add the surcharge and they split it.

GOLD DIGGERS AND GREEN CARD HUNTERS

If a man can break through the gatekeepers at the major dating sites, navigate past their money schemes, and avoid the local scams, he may find himself face to face with a beautiful woman from another country. But now he has to discern the motives and intent of that foreign woman. The biggest concern for many men is that the interest is false and the girl only wants him for his money or just to gain entrance into his country.

Anna has said on several occasions, "Ukrainian women today have many visa options for traveling to other countries. They can go on student visa and tourist or visitor visas. It's ridiculous to think that women today would consider marrying someone just for access to another country. Maybe in the 90's, but not now." Even if this were the case for some, we know that 80% are staying with their men, so it certainly can't be as prominent of a motive as some in the media would want you to believe.

What about the gold diggers? Yes, it's true that many men run in to women who hope to financially gain from dating foreigners. But it's pretty hard to keep up sincerity and avoiding the temptation to ask for money for the entire dating and visa process. You've got at least six months of dating to see if there are any red flags before she will be in your home.

You'll know if her heart is yours long before you bring her home.

CONCLUSION

You've probably already realized that you avoid nearly all of these schemes and concerns by waiting to start your dating overseas until you are there in person. And, if you're only meeting ladies who have been vetted by people you trust then you're in for an enjoyable and sincere experience.

Quit trying to hedge your bets by dating online and trying to sandbag some dates before you go. That mindset is rarely successful, even though it feels like you have more control over the experience.

Take it from the dozens of married couples we've helped to connect: Get offline and get on a plane!

With that behind us, let's move on to one of my all-time favorite topics; attitudes and understandings of masculinity and femininity around the world. Pay attention. These next two chapters could change your life whether you go overseas or not!

BONUS: I've added two bonus videos on this topic:

1. "Scams and the Games of the Mail Order Bride Industry"

2. "CATCH ME IF YOU CAN! Secrets of the Mail Order Bride Industry Revealed"

You'll find both of these linked on the bonuses page at http://www.DreamConnections.com/book

Natalia, age 30

CHAPTER FIVE

MASCULINITY AND FEMININITY

Why is it important to discuss cultural concepts of masculinity and femininity? Before I began traveling abroad, I would never have considered such things. But now I consider them a cornerstone to understanding people.

Without a doubt, there are some basic desires in the hearts of men and women that are true for all of us. It is valuable to understand these so you will be effective when you are trying to win her heart.

Then, there are differences that are culture-based. You will benefit from knowing even a little bit about how the rest of the world views men and women and their roles. You also need to be able to compare that to your culture and be honest with your attitudes and preferences.

Before I go any further, I must also be clear about what I am not talking about. This is not going to be a conversation about "relationships". That will be my next book. This will help you to make more sense of your first interactions.

Before men or women get into any kind of dating or committed relationship with another person, they should first be grounded in their own masculinity or femininity and know where the opposite sex is coming from.

I'm going to try to take a complicated subject and make it as simple as I can. There are two key distinctions in this area of masculinity and femininity: core truths and cultural biases.

As for the core truths, there are some things that are true about men and women because it is hard-wired into our DNA. These things are true for all men and women regardless of their culture or nationality. Unfortunately, much of the "enlightened" Western cultures try to ignore common sense observations about hard-wired, obvious, undeniable differences in men and women and claim that women only play with dolls because of cultural pressures.

If you have not done any reading on the subject then you're in for a wonderful treat. I predict that you are about to enjoy several "aha" moments in the pages ahead. Something will add up and you'll think to yourself, "I've always known that, but I just never put it together before." You are about to be very pleasantly surprised. So let's start by talking about what it means to be a man.

TRUTHS ABOUT MEN AND WOMEN

What I am talking about here comes from extensive research. Much has been written on the topics of defining masculinity and femininity. I have personally studied and researched on the subject of masculinity. I've been a coach and counselor to men for nearly 20 years. I've counseled men who struggle in their relationships with women. I've compared notes with other counselors about the why they think men seem to struggle to understand what it is to be a man. I've been to seminars on dating and understanding women. I also enjoy the comedians who have learned to point out masculine and feminine truth in the most hilarious ways. I have traveled to and dated women in four continents on this earth. I've engaged in conversations with men in those places – often through translators.

From all of these, it became very easy to find the common themes that appeared to be true, even though each may have stated these with different words. The message rose to the top and created a common understanding to help define masculinity and femininity.

I would also encourage you to do some reading on the subject of masculinity for yourself. There have been no books on the subject that have come close to the bestseller status that is held by these two books:

- Iron John, by Robert Bly[6]

- Wild at Heart, by John Eldredge[7]

Combined, they have sold millions of copies and continue to be referenced by those who discuss men's issues.

Iron John is a fascinating study of how previous cultures viewed manliness PRIOR to the industrial revolution. What did it mean to be a man to the ancient cultures of Greece, Germany, Asia, Africa, or Rome? What common rituals survived thousands of years throughout native tribes across different continents? The discussion is laced into a Grimm Brother's story written in 1820. In the introduction, Bly makes this observation, "The grief in men has been increasing steadily since the start of the Industrial Revolution and the grief has reached a depth now that cannot be ignored." You will be enriched for reading it.

Wild at Heart, subtitled, "Discovering the Secret of a Man's Soul" has nearly created a movement of its own. One of the gifts of wisdom is when truth can be made simple to understand. Eldredge does this masterfully. I have never heard the Universal Core of the Masculine Soul and Feminine Soul so beautifully and accurately described as John Eldridge has in his books. He describes the man's heart as having three basic desires. A man needs to have:

- **A Battle to Fight**

- **An Adventure to Live**

- **A Beauty to Pursue**

In a subsequent book he wrote with his wife entitled Captivating, subtitled, "Unveiling the Mystery of the Woman's Soul", they explain the man's heart to the female audience of Captivating this way:

"Every man wants a battle to fight. It's the whole thing with boys and weapons. Just look at the movies men love—Braveheart, Gladiator, Top Gun, High Noon, Saving Private Ryan. Men are made for battle. (And ladies, don't you love the heroes of those movies? You might not want to fight in a war, but don't you long for a man who will fight for you? To have Daniel Day Lewis look you in the eyes and say, "No matter how long it takes . . . no matter how far . . . I will find you"? Women don't fear a man's strength if he is a good man.)

"Men also long for adventure. Adventure is a deeply spiritual longing in the heart of every man. Adventure requires something of us, puts us to the test. Though we may fear the test, at the same time we yearn to be tested, to discover that we have what it takes.

"Finally, every man longs for a beauty to pursue. He really does. Where would Robin Hood be without Marian, or King Arthur without Guinevere? Lonely men fighting lonely battles. You see, it's not just that a man needs a battle to fight. He needs someone to fight for. There is nothing that inspires a man to courage so much as the woman he loves. Most of the daring (and okay, sometimes ridiculous) things young men do are to impress the girls. Men go to war carrying photos of their sweethearts in their wallets—that is a metaphor of this deeper longing to fight for the Beauty. This is not to say that a woman is a "helpless creature" who can't live her life without a man. I'm saying that men long to offer their strength on behalf of a woman.

"Now – can you see how the desires of a man's heart and the desires of a woman's heart were at least meant to fit beautifully together? A woman in the presence of a good man, a real man, loves being a woman. His strength allows her feminine heart to flourish. His pursuit draws out her beauty. And a man in the presence of a real woman loves being a man. Her beauty arouses him to play the man; it draws out his strength. She inspires him to be a hero." [8]

When we ask men the question, "What makes you feel fully alive?" These are the themes. The battles to start a business, beat a competitor, or engage in a political campaign will make a man feel fully alive. You can go white water rafting, camping, hunting, or travel. These can cause us to come alive with adventure. And, the pursuit of a beauty can cause men to expend all of their resources to capture her heart. Winning a good woman's heart can bring all aspects of life to a higher level of exuberance, motivation, and satisfaction.

> *The pursuit of love through international dating is a grand quest that is a battle, an adventure, and a pursuit to rescue the pursue – all wrapped into one. It can bring your heart to life and make you feel fully alive!*

So if the core of masculinity is to have a battle to fight, adventure to live, and a beauty to rescue, then what is the core of the feminine heart?

It is in John Eldredge's book, *Wild at Heart*, that he explains the three aspects of the feminine heart to his male readers. He says that the feminine heart:

- Wants to be pursued

- Wants to be caught up in an adventure

• Wants to have beauty she can unveil

Eldredge describes it this way:

"Not every woman wants a battle to fight, but every woman yearns to be fought for. Listen to the longing of a woman's heart: She wants to be more than noticed – she wants to be wanted. She wants to be pursued.

"I just want to be a priority to someone," a friend in her 30s told me. And her childhood dreams of a knight in shining armor coming to rescue her are not girlish fantasies; they are the core of the feminine heart and the life she knows she was made for. So Zach comes back for Paula in An Officer and a Gentleman, Frederick comes back for Jo in Little Women, and Edward returns to pledge his undying love for Eleanor in Sense and Sensibility.

"Every woman also wants an adventure to share. One of my wife's favorite films is The Man from Snowy River. She loves the scene where Jessica, the beautiful young heroine, is rescued by Jim, her hero, and together they ride on horseback through the wilds of the Australian wilderness. "I want to be Isabo in Ladyhawk," confessed another female friend. "To be cherished, pursued, fought for – yes. But also, I want to be strong and a part of the adventure." So many men make the mistake of thinking that the woman is the adventure. But that is where the relationship immediately goes downhill. A woman doesn't want to be the adventure; she wants to be caught up into something greater than herself. One friend went on to say, "I know myself and I know I'm not the adventure. So when a man makes me the point, I grow bored immediately. I know that story. Take me into one I don't know."

"And finally, every woman wants to have a beauty to unveil. Not to conjure, but to unveil. Most women feel the pressure to be beautiful from very young, but that is not what I speak of. There is also a deep desire to simply and truly be the beauty, and be delighted in. Most little girls will remember playing dress up, or wedding day, or "twirling skirts." Those flowing dresses that were perfect for spinning around in. She'll put her pretty dress on, come into the living room and twirl. What she longs for is to capture her daddy's delight. My wife remembers standing on top of the coffee table as a girl of five or six and singing her heart out. "Do you see me?" asks the heart of every girl. And, "Are you captivated by what you see?""[9]

I have become fascinated by the energy that can come from the connection of these two hearts. Napoleon's men felt empowered when Josephine was with them in the battle camp. They know that their captain felt invincible because of the way she loved and empowered him. When the church stepped in and refused to allow her to come to him on the battlefield, Napoleon lacked that cutting edge – that eye of the tiger – and their victory was in question.

What is that dynamic about? What did she do for him? What made him want to win for her and feel invincible when he knew she would be waiting for him in his tent upon his return from battle?

I have tried to capture this dynamic in a poem I wrote called "The Radiant Passions." In it I describe what is going on in the heart of the man and woman in the format of a story/poem. Each character in the poem is strong and intelligent. They understand the strength, power and influence they carry.

THE RADIANT PASSIONS

By Mark Edward Davis

The woman I treasure carries ecstatic love in her eyes.

She passes this way and every man turns his head in hopes of a stolen glance.

The object of her gaze, even caught in passing, becomes less of this world and more radiant – transcending.

When a man hears her voice, sweet and true, the things of earth lose their taste and dim.

And when she smiles at him, even for an instant, there comes a feeling – a blissful sensation granted to men by angels and oft materialized in the laughter of children.

From his chest glows a mysterious passion to serve - to find a quest - to stand on a champion's podium victorious.

The radiant power of glance, voice and smile demand a noble quest worthy of the passion within.

This passion, radiating from his core, is more than ample to the quest.

The wild man and his inner warriors engage the fight - the golden ball is his rightful prize

The woman, gazing upon the conquering man, finds herself overwhelmed by a new glow radiating from within her breast.

She approaches the victor's podium and chooses the man as the object of her passion - a noble passion of its own - a golden ball with her name inscribed.

Then the woman with ecstatic love in her eyes passes this way on the arm of her champion.

There is no logic of earth to explain this miracle – splendid, radiant, amazing, mysterious and new.

It just is - has been - and will be for all time true.

I was inspired by various themes from Iron John in writing this poem. There he discusses the "golden ball" as a symbol from Ancient Greek culture, which represents true fulfillment of the soul's desire. The inner wild men are a resource men have within them to go to battle and risk to do things that are bigger than themselves. In Iron John, Bly also translates a poem from Dante, which echoed these truths.

The woman brings the man's heart to life – stirring power, strength, and masculinity in his soul. He wants to do something for her to show her who he is. She knows she is beautiful and enjoys the energy of flirting. But in the end, she wants to be the woman on the arm of a champion.

I say these things to help prepare you for the posture that will make you radiantly attractive. To put it into one sentence, here is your posture, "I am a king who is traveling the world in search of his queen." You have accomplished things in life. You have found success. You have accumulated enough finances to be able to travel and support your queen. It is your time to grace your castle, and your kingdom, with the radiant power of a beautiful queen.

These are the core truths that I wanted to communicate to you. Everything else is culture and personal preference.

Elena, age 30

CHAPTER SIX

CULTURAL DIFFERENCES FOR MEN AND WOMEN

In America, we truly are out of touch with cultures and attitudes abroad. Most men here have not done a lot of traveling around the world. I wish they all would. Consider the impact it would have on your world perspective to actually visit the diverse cultures from Australia, China, Japan, Brazil, Germany, Denmark, Russia, to Egypt.

I'm sure you have probably watched movies filmed in places all over the world. You most likely feel you would know what to expect if you went to one of those countries. But that all goes to another level when you are there and you have to communicate with locals.

I am completely fascinated to get inside the thought process of other cultures. So many people are just like you and me – yet they see things from such a different perspective. Not only does it help me understand them better, but it helps give perspective to my world view.

In the last chapter we took a look at the healthy masculinity and femininity and how they complement and energize each other. It is this euphoric energy that we're all looking for.

Now we'll look at some of the weaker sides of our cultures. We'll compare the way we look at things like sex, money, and family. We'll look at some of the problems in the lives of men and women abroad. Then we'll take a look at some areas that are problematic for men and women in our country.

COMPARING CULTURAL DIFFERENCES OF MEN AROUND THE WORLD

FIRST: FOREIGN MEN

I have enjoyed spending time with some of the men I met overseas. The guys who hosted sail fishing in Costa Rica were awesome to hang with. I really enjoyed the humor of one of the cab drivers in Rio de Janeiro. These guys can be a blast to be around.

But there also seems to be some deep seeded pains and struggles in their lives. The way they react to the social and economic traps of life in their countries brings out the worst in many of them when it comes to their love lives.

Government statistics, from countries such as Russia and Columbia, tend to support the statements I heard from so many women. Alcoholism and spousal abuse is prevalent. As a lifestyle, many foreign men spend much of their time with other men conversing, smoking, and drinking. Women are often just the objects of sexual conquest – and sometimes abused. These women will say that men in the younger generations are not seeing the motivation for getting married – especially when they can have new sex partners on a regular basis.

To further feed the situation, foreign women will do whatever they can in an attempt to keep them. Most foreign women have little expectation that their man will remain faithful to them but will fight to keep him anyway.

There's a growing number of women who are fed up with this game and want no part of it. For them, hope of having a loving family with a good man in their own country has become a remote possibility.

Obviously, this harsh picture is not true of all men. I met several married couples that seemed very happy with each other – but I didn't talk to the men alone to hear their attitudes toward marriage or uncover any philandering. But even among these married men, the sense of economic frustration had set in – they just can't make more money for themselves or their families in an emerging or socialist society.

One of the reasons foreign men may pursue the conquest of one woman after another is to fill a huge void in their lives. Men are built to have a battle to fight – metals of accomplishment to win. What if you lived in a world where you could never advance or make any more money than you did when you were 20 years old? Would you spend half of your time killing your pain with smoking and alcohol? Wouldn't you be looking to find other non-economic places that you could battle and win – and prove your manhood? Thus, the conquest of more women may be one of those battles. But these victories have no honor.

Another painful fallout from masculinity gone wrong is domestic abuse. The overblown male machismo culture of domination and physical abuse is considered common in Latin America and Asia – yet rarely punished.

Apparently, many of these men seem to find little motivation to bring their paychecks home – even when they have a monogamous relationship and children. The common story seems to be that the women work so the family has money.

What is the consequence for this lifestyle? According to CIA world statistics, the average life expectancy for men is 59 in Russia, 62 in Ukraine, and 65 in Colombia. Alcohol is a major contributing factor to these shortened life spans. 4

SECOND: MEN FROM THE WEST

At first glance, those men make us look like heroes by contrast. Modern Western men want to be connected with their families. We participate in our wives pregnancies and delivery. We change diapers and teach our kids to play baseball. We take our wives on dates and plan our vacations as family events. We want to be faithful to our wives, because this is what good husbands do. To have an affair also means we failed in our marriages somehow. We desire closeness and intimacy with our women. These are good and noble aspirations.

Our families come first and we bring home our entire paychecks to support our family. We don't abuse our spouses or children. And we lavish upon them the highest standard of living in the modern age.

But, as men in the West, we have also had to deal with cultural influences that have pushed us in the opposite direction of our foreign counterparts: toward the feminine-first perspective. I've never spoken to a Western man who denied that there are pressures in their culture that attack masculinity. Even if we have held strong to our manliness, we live under the threat of losing our jobs over unfounded suggestions of sexual harassment in the workplace. In order to get a college degree we are forced to take "women's studies" and "gender sensitivity" classes. What do these courses teach? They teach that men are sexual predators and the cause of every historic evil on the planet – and that we fill all of the prisons – not women.

Robert Bly describes the affects of various decades of American history on men in his book, "Iron John." Here is what he said about the decade of the 1960's:

> "During the sixties, another sort of man appeared. As men began to examine women's history and women's sensibility, some men began to notice what was called their feminine side and pay attention to it. This process continues to this day, and I would say that most contemporary men are involved in it in some way.

. . . The male in the past twenty years has become more thoughtful, more gentle. But by this process he has not become more free. He's a nice boy who pleases not only his mother, but also the young woman he is living with.

In the seventies I began to see all over the country a phenomenon that we might call the "soft male." They are lovely, valuable people – I like them – they're not interested in harming the earth or starting wars. There's a gentle attitude toward life in their whole being and style of living.

But many of these men are not happy. You quickly notice the lack of energy in them. They are life-preserving, but not exactly life-giving. Ironically, you often see these men with strong women who positively radiate energy." [9]

If you look at the Western society in a worldview, we have changed our understanding of masculinity in ways that clearly lean toward the feminine. It is out of balance. Some men are also soft when it comes to romance. We may send flowers and take them to dinner, but never really move to win their hearts, offer them our strength, or take them away on an adventure.

I know that when I saw a beautiful woman in the past I would become flustered and starry-eyed. I felt inferior and "out of my league". I gave away too much of my masculine presence and was far too easily impressed. Now I see this as weakness; even though our culture may have taught us that this is romantic and flattering to the woman. In truth, they see it as weakness as well.

I'm not so worried that you are a feminized man. The fact that you are reading this book tells me that you have a heart for adventure. You are not willing to settle for less than the best. If you take the challenge to find love abroad, you will have moved on to a higher plain. You are a man of action.

You are going to find it easy to get the attention of gorgeous women on your trip. I just want you to be able to understand where they are coming from. They don't need you to go ga-ga over them. They want to meet a kind-hearted man with a good sense of humor, but they want to meet a man. You need to be keenly aware of the indoctrination you've been immersed in from our culture toward the feminized men.

The women overseas are accustomed to seeing strong men – in fact – overbearing and brutal men. They would love to meet a "good" strong man. That's what they're looking for. They want to find a man with kindness in his heart – and one who will pursue her to win her heart, provide for her, and protect her.

The purpose of masculinity is to offer our strength to world. In this case, you are the knight in shining armor – and you are looking for a beauty to rescue. Or, more appropriately, *you are a king who is searching the world to find his queen.*

COMPARING CULTURAL DIFFERENCES OF WOMEN AROUND THE WORLD

It is invigorating to be around a woman who is strong and has found joy in being a woman – the healthy feminine soul. As I said in my poem, they are radiant.

I believe that all women have the potential to be radiant and reveal their own beauty. Even when Oprah was extremely overweight, she loved herself, dressed well, and radiated with feminine beauty and energy. This is first, and foremost, and internal beauty. Although we, as men, will place physical beauty high on our list of desirable traits, it falls to second place when we consider the highest state of love is the romantic connection that sets our souls ablaze. Our heart's desire is to find the best of both; beauty inside and out.

The advantage you will have with international dating is that nearly all of your prospective dates would be 8's to 10's by beauty standards in your country. That box is checked off even before you arrive. Your sorting process is really about finding the one you have a powerful connection with.

What are the challenges facing women? Let's talk about the foreign women first.

FIRST: FOREIGN WOMEN

Most of the women you will meet on one of these Quest Tours have had to struggle and work hard in life. Many of them have been working since they were 15-years-old. Yet they have not only finished school, but also added university education in and around their work schedules. They are proud of their hard work and personal accomplishments so they might have the best possible future.

As we discussed before, it is very competitive for one of these women to find a good man. Therefore, when they do have a man in their lives, they will focus on pleasing him – and they truly do take pleasure when they can make him happy.   In this competitive environment they often become skilled in seduction and sensuality within the relationship. They work hard to keep him focused on her so he has no reason to look around. I still find it cute that my gorgeous younger wife watches out for other women who might be looking at me!

They continually work on their looks. They dress well and tend to stay fit. This is especially true for both men and women in Asia and Eastern Europe. They may only have a few outfits, but they will always look the best they can. That is one reason you want to be dressed well – and in fashion – when you meet these ladies for the first time.

Workweeks are often six days, not five. They don't have labor laws as we do, so breaks are fewer and further between. They may work a 50 to 60 hour week and take home less than $400 per month US equivalent. But it is this life of struggle that has given them maturity at earlier ages than we would typically find in your country.

My friend Steve wondered what I would have to talk about with a 20-year plus age difference between my wife and I. That concern was completely removed once Anna arrived in the US and Steve got to spend some time with her. He is still captivated by her understanding of people and life strategies. She is more than capable of engaging in any conversation we might have – and often surprises us with her candid insights.

But the most delightful thing about these women is their resilient spirits. They find laughter and happiness in the life they have been given. This was the same life their mother and grandmother had, so who are they to complain? It would be an insult to their family. If they do find a good man, even one abroad, their family at home will most likely be glad for them; but only if he makes her truly happy.

These women are traditional in that they do not ask men out on dates or flirt excessively. The men are the pursuers and the initiators. They believe in the man being the head of the home. These are classy, elegant women who deserve to be treated like you would as if you were going on a date with a hot TV reporter from your local news station. They are educated and gorgeous; yet traditional in the way they see family and marriage.

In our country, women might see that brand of traditional attitude as weak. Don't underestimate these women. The only thing missing from their lives, as they see it, is romantic attention. Otherwise, they are generally satisfied with their lives. They don't need you to save them and take them away from a horrible life of poverty. That is not the way they view their world and would be insulted if you were to suggest such a thing. But, give them romantic attention and treat them like you were trying to win their heart; and you just may. The reward is a deep and richly satisfying relationship.

SECOND: WOMEN FROM THE WEST

You and I may be on a different path for the simple reason that we've had bad personal experiences with women. Yet, at the same time, we have all had relationships with some local women we loved. The poem I wrote entitled "The Radiant Passions" was originally written for an American woman who captured my imagination and inspired creativity in me. I'm not saying there aren't any prospects of finding a good woman in your own country. I have been completely captivated by women in my country on several occasions in my life.

But my heart goes out to Western women – it really does. It is my opinion that they have been fed the "Superwoman" standard for performance too long and they are experiencing burnout. The standards held up for Western women include competing with men in business, raising children, keeping up with domestic chores at home, and giving back to their communities. These women grow up expecting to carry the roles of both men and women and keep themselves beautiful all at the same time.

Paula Cole sings, "Where have all the cowboys gone?" And yet women in our modern societies are being taught that they need to be the cowboy, cowgirl, sheriff, and showgirl all in one.

No one can be all things to all people. *Something has to give!*

For some women, they give up on being the showgirl – they stop paying attention to their beauty – and stop trying to seduce their man. Some will just stay in the cowboy role. Strong women can thrive as business executives and become the dominating partners in marriage. If they keep some aspects of the showgirl it may be done to help advance their cowboy agenda in the workplace; but their heart is in the roping, tying and branding. Other women may just latch on to the showgirl and use their sex appeal to land their sugar daddy. Finally, there are others who latch on to the cowgirl role to the exclusion of all else – becoming isolated into domestic life.

I should stop for a moment to consider one thought: perhaps these women are genuinely happy with these roles. Maybe it works for them. After all, the great advantage of a free society is choice – you can be whatever you want to be.

Personally, I enjoy seeing femininity come to life in the combined roles of cowgirl and showgirl – to keep with the analogy. The cowgirl does not try to run the ranch, but rides along side her cowboy as they make their ranch into what they dream it to be together. She seduces him almost daily with her showgirl appeal to encourage his masculinity and empower him as Josephine did with Napoleon.

This combination seems to be the norm for foreign woman. She desires to support her man in his ambitions and empower him with praise and affection. In the heart of a good man, it creates a desire to fight battles for her, shower her with love, and adorn her with the good things in life. The woman who will lavishly support her man with affection and admiration will have no difficulty drawing out of him these desires and benefit from the rewards.

So how is it possible for men and women in Western societies to create marriages that will work with such diverse expectations? It is hard indeed. The statistics are that less than half find a way to even stay married, not to mention finding deep satisfaction and enduring love.

Answer this question for yourself right now: How many good marriages do you know? By that I mean the kind of relationships that make you envious of what they have – a companionship and passion you wish you had. How many would you answer? I've done this survey many times over the past five years and the results are always the same. Just over 60% will answer "0" or "1". So what's your role model for a good marriage?

This may be hard medicine to swallow, but I want you to evaluate the reality of your situation and listen to what it is telling you. Maybe this path of looking for love in your own country isn't working for a reason.

I'm sure that there are many women where you live who have loving and kind hearts. Don't you think that these women want to have deep and meaningful connections in the way we've discussed? Of course they do. Perhaps they too are just looking for love in all the wrong places.

I can't answer for them – or you. We're each on our own path. I am simply a man who is eternally grateful to have found such a deep and richly satisfying love relationship – and I stand in the company of other men who have found the same – in the same place I did. We just wish this kind of happiness for you – wherever you find it – home or abroad.

Men like us have struggled to find ways to live out adventures and find a beauty to rescue (or one that wants to be rescued). While in other parts of the world there are women who are not finding men who will pursue their hearts and take them away on a grand adventure. Both are left with places of emptiness and little hope that their situations will change – little hope that they will find a life that makes their hearts come fully alive.

That's why I truly believe that we are a perfect – and natural fit – between the good masculine men in the West and these wonderful foreign ladies. It's like a match made in heaven. If I were to boil this all down to a simple idea it would be this: If you are going to pour your heart into the love of a woman – you just want to know that she is going to pour that much energy back into loving you. As my friend Steve summarized it, "Mark, I just want you to find a woman who will match your efforts".

Most of these foreign women are willing to pour their lives into the love of a good man – and they want to find someone who will pour themselves back into loving her. What I have found is that the energy between the Golden Man and his foreign wife is growing and dynamic. Their love and willingness to give to each other creates an ongoing momentum that continues to feed both. They actually feel *more* in love as time goes by.

If you find what you are reading rings a chord of truth – that it somehow resonates in your heart – then it's time for you to take action and make your move.

BONUS: Anna and I went through the "10 Most Frequently Observed Uniqueness's with Ukrainian Women" and captured her unique perspective in a live Q&A video session. Catch this video on the Bonus page at this link: http://www.DreamConnections.com/book

Jeremy and Gala
married in Canada
after meeting on a
Quest Tour

CHAPTER SEVEN

DATING OVERSEAS:
A FIRST-PERSON WALKTHROUGH

Once you've stepped onto a plane in the pursuit of your queen, you have joined the ranks of the top 3% of men – the "Men of Action" who broke free from their computer screens and experienced the adventure for themselves!

The day has come and you are ready to step on to that plane. The moment you do, you become part of that top 3% who took action. We know, statistically speaking, that 97% of the men who join an international dating website never go anywhere beyond their computers. They're stuck – but you're not! You are part of an elite group of international daters – the men of action. Welcome to the club!

It's an amazing experience that I will walk you through shortly. But first, I have to enjoy this moment with you.

I am a man who is married to the most amazing women I could have possibly imagined! No, I don't think I could have even imagined how wonderful it has been to be in relationship with my Ukrainian wife, Anna. She's a brilliant woman who keeps me feeling young and alive. She has a life and vibrancy about her that is hard to explain. She adds joy, entertainment, and sensual stimulation to my life each day. I also love the attention she draws from other men here in America, because she is so beautiful. I know her heart is mine so I can just bask in the 'eat-your-hearts-out' glow without any jealousy. She loves flashing her wedding ring at them. She daily reminds me that she loves me and that she is mine.

Often a guy will ask, "Does she have a sister?" To which I reply, "Yes, thousands of them!"

But they'll never find out if they don't get on a plane and go on the quest for themselves. But once you do, you and I become kindred spirits in a very small club of guys who DO know something the rest may never know.

So, I say again, *welcome to the club!*

ADVANCE TRAINING FOR YOUR EXPERIENCE

I now require all clients to go through six training videos I've titled, "Winning Strategies for Dating Foreign Women". We've seen dramatic improvement in men's success rates when they've gone through these. The six videos cover each of these topics:

1. First Impressions

2. Pacing and Timing

3. Perfect Dates

4. Working with your Team

5. Closing the Deal

6. Riding Into the Sunset

7. Bonus Video: How to Tell if a Foreign Women is "In to You"

We've had so many tell us that the education made all the difference for them, so it became the first of our core beliefs: More Education = More Success. You'll know what the ladies are hoping to find in a man. You'll feel much more confident in what to do and realistically expect on your journey. And you'll be more relaxed and enjoy the experience so much more.

Once you arrive and set foot on foreign soil, you will get the first chance to meet up with your tour host and the other guys you'll be sharing the adventure with. You are all now part of that International Dating fraternity - even before you have met one girl in person. There is a buzz of excitement and expectation among the men in the group.

If you haven't traveled overseas very much, the flights may have seemed long, but their also invigorating because you know that it means you're actually doing it. All of your senses are alive with anticipation.

I do want to offer some tips regarding the air travel. There will most likely be one leg of your flight that is 8 to 12 hours in length. It's important to get some sleep on this flight if at all possible, so creating a plan for your time in flight is helpful. My first recommendation is that you get an aisle seat so you don't have to crawl over anyone to get up and down. Plan on watching a movie when you first take off. The first big meal will be served about 90 minutes into your flight. Finish the movie and do whatever works for you to try to get 4 to 6 hours of sleep. Then watch another movie and know that the second major meal will come about 90 minutes before landing. Having a schedule of what to do and expect makes the time go by quickly and allows you to land feeling refreshed.

Once you land at your destination city you will be met by someone from the company as soon as you come out of baggage claim. You're never alone or have to worry about how you'll get to the hotel. The staff member will already have a car waiting and will take you to the hotel and to join up with the rest of the guys. If you've chosen to join a Dream Connections' Quest Tour, and I'll presume you have, then you're fired up to finally meet some of the men you've been interacting with in your tour's secret Facebook group. Many of the guys in the group already feel like they know each other – and now you get to finally meet in person.

If you'd like to take the lessons from this book and apply them to a different system or method for dating overseas you're more than welcome to. My whole purpose is to help more men succeed. I just believe that you'll need to adapt the strategies we use on Quest Tour into the method you plan on using in order to have your best chance for success.

Now that you are on foreign soil, be aware of the magic of your surroundings. You are in a new country you may have never been to before – and who knows when you'll be back again. Build the fascination with this culture even now. Having conversations about her country will be much easier on your dates if you are genuinely interested and have noticed things you could ask her about.

DATING OVERSEAS: A FIRST-PERSON WALK-THROUGH

I've always said that the best thing you can do for yourself before going overseas is to have a vivid and accurate picture of what your experience is going to be like so you'll feel like you've already been there when you arrive. It's the same thing astronauts and pilots do with simulations – so allow me to help provide you with the best simulation I can in the pages ahead.

BONUS: In May of 2014 I captured the first-person perspective of a Quest Tour on my iPhone. It doesn't get more authentic than this. You'll find it labeled "Video Journal" at this page: http://www.DreamConnections.com/book.

For the sake of this simulation, I'm going to take you through the Quest Tour Experience; although I'm sure you'll get a clear enough picture of what it's like to serve you whether you go on a Quest Tour or not. Here we go!

THE DAY YOU ARRIVE

The plane touches down at an airport like most others you've been to, just a bit smaller. You grab your overhead bag and walk down the ramp they pulled up next to the plane and board a bus that takes you to the terminal. You get in line to show your passport to a customs agent and then wait at the carousel to grab your luggage. As you walk out the door from baggage claim you see a familiar face holding up a "Dream Connections" sign waiting for you. He smiles and greets you by name. You sigh with relief. It's all good.

He grabs your bags and you jump in the car he has waiting and start to drive from the airport through the city. It feels familiar in some ways and different in others. You think to yourself, "I did it. I'm really here".

The driver lets you know that he's taking you to the hotel to check in and then you have the option to take a nap or catch up with the rest of the guys, who are having lunch at a pizza place next to the downtown park. Right now you are so glad you decided to come on Thursday, a day before the official program begins. There's no rush and plenty of time to get adjusted. "Let's check in and then join the guys. There are a couple of them I can't wait to meet in person."

After checking in you meet up with a few of the other guys who came early. You've been chatting with these guys on the secrete Facebook group for a few weeks and you feel like you've just joined a reunion. They already start talking about how many gorgeous women they've seen everywhere they've been. It's all real – and just like the videos said it would be. It feels like déjà vu – in a good way!

Marina, the local manager for Dream Connections, joins the group and offers to host a walking tour of the city for those who are up to it. Some join in and others head back to the hotel to take a nap.

This was a great first day.

FRIDAY EVENT:
MEET YOUR PERSONAL ASSISTANT DINNER

The first official day of the Quest Tour is here. Breakfast at the hotel was leisurely. You decided to walk around town some more and enjoy the great weather. The rest of the men have arrived, each one picked up at the airport, and it's finally time for the first event, the Meet Your Personal Assistant Dinner Event.

As you walk in the front door of the restaurant you see themes all around the room that reflect the culture of the country. It's a way to get you introduced to traditional foods as a backdrop for the week. One by one each man is introduced to his personal assistant/translator and now it's your turn. "This is Elena", the host says and she introduces you. You are amazed. She's such a beautiful young woman: graceful, professional, and charming. When you take your seats at one of the tables you can't help but wonder if she's single too!

Elena takes out a folder from her purse and starts going through the photos of all the ladies who have confirmed to be attending the events that weekend. Wow again! This is going to be awesome!

As the evening goes on, you enjoy an amazing meal and share your life story with your new best friend. She asks more about the type of lady you're hoping to meet so she can refine her intuition for you.

As you head back to the hotel you're sense of comfort grows to excitement. This is awesome.

Your translator is your partner for the week, your date planner, B.S. detector, and new best friend.

SATURDAY EVENT:
"MEET & MATCH EVENT" DAY ONE

The day begins with breakfast on the patio of the hotel café as you watch the city come alive and people walking back and forth in front of you. You can't help but notice the lovely ladies in high heals walking by on their way to who knows where.

10:00am rolls around and it's time for Mark's first coaching session. He talks about how to work with your translator and to be sure to shake the hands of each lady at each table before you sit down. He talks about the types of questions they'll be asking and more about the format for the day. "You're not trying to date them today – you're just spending a bit to time to see if there was a spark with someone that makes you want to spend another hour with her," Mark says. "Remember that 'laughter leads to love' and pay attention to the ones who share your humor. If there was one that jumped out to you then have your translator ask her if she's available right after the event. Seize the day!"

The session breaks and you wait in the on the café patio with your translator. Anna Davis is at the restaurant seating the ladies. When she feels the timing is right, she'll give the word and everyone gets on the bus to head to the restaurant for the first Meet & Match Event.

YOUR FIRST MEET & MATCH EVENT

Your assistant and new best friend, Elena, has a list of the tables and what order you'll rotate through each. You walk in the room to see a dozen tables with lovely ladies seated at each. You can't help but scan the room to take it all in. TV monitors around the room show photos of married couples that met on previous Quest Tours. Tables have fruit plates on each and you can faintly hear soft music in the background just to add some good energy to the room.

You approach the first table and greet three local ladies. They came dressed for a nice event and their smiles are warm. You start off by introducing yourself and sharing a little about what you do and the city you live in. Then they start asking questions:

- Is it your first time in to our country?

- What do you think of our city?

- What are your hobbies?

- Do you have brothers or sisters?

- Why are you looking overseas?

- Have you been in a serious relationship before?

- Do you have children? Do you want children?

Fortunately, you went through all of Mark's training videos and you understand where the ladies are coming from and you have fun with your answers. In fact, it was really fun to turn things around and ask them a few questions.

It was amazing how they could ask such direct questions, but seemed so sincere when they asked. You didn't sense any games – just honest curiosity. It was amazing to see how they focused on you without being distracted. This is nothing like you've experienced before!

The Dream Connections' manager says you have one minute left at this table. Wow! That was a quick 15 minutes! You wrap up the conversations and shake each ladies hand again. When you get up from the table you mention to Elena that you liked one of the girls, Victoria, and wanted to see if she would go out later in the week. She says OK, and sits back down at the table while you go hang with the other guys for a minute before the next round starts. Elena asks the ladies if any of them would like to go out on a date with you to please write their phone numbers on her card. Two of the three do, including Victoria!

OK, you've got this down now. You approach the next table with Elena and greet the ladies warmly and start with your introduction again.

This is repeated through another four tables, and then an awesome meal is served while at the next table. By the end of the day you've got nearly 15 phone numbers and 8 of them were on your "YES" list. Before you leave, Elena finds Victoria and asks her if she is available to do something with you that night. She is and you are higher than a kite!

The three of you walk out together and take a stroll along the river front to a totally cool café by the water. You're date is petite, long hair, high heels, and graceful. She shares stories about her life and seems so fascinated with yours. This is amazing.

SUNDAY:
MEET & MATCH EVENT DAY TWO

You wake up to another beautiful day and enjoy the breakfast and café patio again. Elena called several of the other ladies you asked about who gave their phone numbers and now you've already got 4 more dates lined up.

10:00am comes around and Mark's coaching today is more of a question and answer session from all of the events the day before. But they men are feeling more relaxed and excited now that they have an idea of how everything works – and they've thought of more great responses to questions and things they'd like to ask. Everyone is ready to go, but Mark offers this one additional bit of advice, "Men, when you do have a date that is going well, and you're really enjoying her company, don't let her leave your presence without setting up the time for your next date together. She knows that you're going to be going out on other dates, but as long as she knows she has you again at 2:00 on Tuesday then you are not losing momentum with her – and it allows you to do what you came to do." Great advice. Now I need for Elena to call

Victoria right away to set up our follow up date so she doesn't feel left behind.

The Meet & Match Event today operates with the same format, but all of the girls are new – no repeats from the day before. By the end of this day you have another 20 phone numbers and a new set of six that are at the top of your list!

MONDAY THROUGH THURSDAY

As the week goes on, you develop a rhythm with Elena. You have three dates set for Monday, four for Tuesday, and a repeat with Victoria for Wednesday morning.

Each date is a little different. Elena keeps things interesting for you and your dates. On one date you go to the zoo and another you shoot billiards. Mark recommends that every date have two components: a time to sit across a table and learn about your date, and then something physical to do – even if that's just a walk through the park. It's a great strategy and Elena has lots of ideas of things to do in town.

For second dates she suggests getting more creative. You bring flowers and have a picnic on a chartered 25' sail boat you hired just for your date. The cost was only $20US per hour because the currency exchange rate is so favorable. This opens up a lot of possibilities. On another date you go horseback riding. On another occasion, when your morning was completely free, Elena took you to see one of the local museums.

Once or twice during the week there have been times when Mark & Anna get the group back together to take a night off and have fun. No dates. It's time to relax with the guys and translators and just hang out for a while.

You've completely forgotten what your other life was like.

By Thursday you have had four dates with Victoria and the last two were four and five hours long each. You found what you came to find. She has been showing you all of the signs Mark talked about in his presentation on how to know if a foreign women is "in to you". This is starting to feel magical!

BONUS: To watch the presentation "How To Tell if a Foreign Woman is "In To You"" go to http://www.DreamConnections.com/book and on the bonuses page you'll see the link.

FRIDAY:
PROM NIGHT DINNER EVENT

By the end of the week, most of the men have found one lady that rose to the top and the two of them are very excited – some are even giddy with excitement. The Prom Night Dinner Event is a finale event for the week. It's held at a very romantic restaurant and now is when you get to see which man has been connecting with which lady.

The scenery is gorgeous and you ask the photographer to get some special photos of you and Victoria together to celebrate your meeting each other. Later, you'll frame one of those photos to leave with her as a keepsake.

DEPARTING FOR HOME

This is what you were hoping you'd experience when you came. Once you get home, you'll follow the path to get to know Victoria better and see if she truly is the life-partner you were hoping to meet. No matter what comes of it, it was the experience of a lifetime and it's all good.

Nearly half of the men were able to make arrangements to stay a few extra days to deepen the new relationships they've started, but you've got to get to work on Monday. Victoria has made a special effort to be available to ride with you to the airport to see you off. The two of you have been exchanging cute pictures from your phones through Viber. You've set up a time when you'll Skype with each other once you get home. And you've made arrangements for her to take English language classes at the Dream Connections' office starting next week.

The time has been magical. Your friendship with Elena has been very personal and very special. After all, who else has ever sat through dates with you! The guys have formed a bond and many will be friends for life.

Anna Astafieva is now Anna Davis.

We met on December 10, 2006 and were married on
October 13, 2007.

CHAPTER EIGHT

MY STORY OF MEETING ANNA

First, I must start by stating the obvious: Dream Connections did not exist at the time I went to Ukraine and met my wife. I went with a different company that had a different model for hosting what they called, "socials" and "romance tours". In their model you go to one city and attend a social where 200 to 300 ladies are in a large banquet room.

There was no organization to the event. You did not have an assigned translator. You had to get up the courage to just sit at a table with women and hope at least one of them spoke some English. There were typically six to eight women at a table. There were translators available somewhere in the room, but you had to go find one if you wanted to use one at a table, so you spent most of your time just talking with English speaking ladies. After two hours they turned the room into a nightclub, dimmed the lights, and cranked up the music.

Additionally, they had no idea who these ladies were except that their local affiliate agencies invited them. In the very first city on my romance tour I met a gorgeous, petite blond named Anastasia. I ended spending my first day and a half with her – my entire time in Odessa. She sweet talked me into buying her jewelry and then offered herself to me for $400. Wow.

My other beef with this other system is that they take you to three different cities in 9 days. You spend two days at each city and then return to the first city for the final days. So, if you started to build a connection with a woman in one city you had to excuse yourself to stay with the group and leave to go to another city. And she knows where you're going – to date more women. You're dead in the water.

One reason letter-writing through these online websites is so critical to their clients is that the men can set up some dates for themselves in advance with the women they have written to and not have to rely on who shows up at the socials. So it was with me and two ladies: Kristina and Tatyana.

Earlier in Chapter 3 I mentioned the letters I exchanged with Kristina. She was the one who asked what a woman could do to make me happy every day. Well, we continued writing and agreed to meet in Nikolaev, which was the next city on this romance tour. Based on the depth of letters that we'd exchanged, I had high hopes that Kristina would be "the one".

When we got to the next town and we walked into the disco where the social was being held, I immediately found one of the agency staff and asked about her. Soon we were sitting at a table just the two of us. She looked every bit as beautiful as her pictures. I wasn't sure what to say. My expectations were so high that I was quite nervous. Eventually, we started to talk, but she kept watching the door looking for a friend of hers to arrive.

This was certainly not the magic I was expecting would happen between us. Maybe it was all on my side. But how could that be true when she wrote such wonderful things in her letters?

Then she dropped the bomb on me. She said her work was far away from the agency and she didn't have time to answer all of my letters so she asked the agency translators to reply to my letters for her. She could only recall the very first one I wrote. She had zero emotional connection with me – and I thought I'd be marrying this girl. Ouch.

I was completely taken back. I didn't know how to respond. In retrospect I guess I should have asked to meet the translator (if it wasn't a man)! I excused myself and wished her a wonderful evening, but it took me more than an hour to recover.

The dancing started so I decided I'd just find someone to dance with and try to shake it off. I danced with this adorable blond girl who had fantastic energy. I left her for a moment to get a drink of water and one of the other guys started dancing with the blond girl – and never left her side.

I moped for a little longer and then realized that there were only 20 minutes left in the entire event – and I didn't even have one date lined up!   I was not about to end up dateless.

I decided that I had to find someone to spend some time with – and it mattered even less who it was at this point.   I scanned the room for someone who looked interesting that I hadn't connected with yet.   From the upper level I could see all the way across the room to two girls who were in the back corner sitting by themselves. And I knew they weren't there earlier.   Well, they looked cute from 100 feet away and they were alone so I marched toward them, passing across the dance floor as I went.

I walked up to the table and said, "Hi, I'm Mark," in a cheery, yet relaxed voice.   They both appeared to be in their early to mid-20's and very lovely indeed.   One was blond and the other a red head.   The blond answered first, "I'm Anna."   Then the red head chimed in, "and I'm Anna."

"You're both Anna?" I asked.   They both smiled and nodded.   "Whew.   I've had a long day and that will make it much easier on me tonight.   Thank you!"   They both laughed.

Since the "party" was nearly over, I decided to go ahead and ask them both out right then and there, "I have never been to your city before and I have no plans for this evening.   Would you mind if I just took both of you out to dinner tonight?   I'd love to just walk through your city and let you show me what there is to see.   It just sounded like a better way to end the day."

They looked at each other and gladly agreed. Can you just see me now as I walked out that door with one beautiful woman on each arm! We walked through the streets and they told me about the statues and the main street. We ended up at a wonderful sushi restaurant that overlooked the town square.

Anna Red, as I called her – had a very animated personality and made conversation easy. Anna Blond was more reserved, but her smile captivated me. Her eyes told me that there was a deeper soul lurking below the surface. At some point during dinner I just felt a captivating connection to Anna-Blond – one that I still find hard to describe. It was like an electrical attraction – a bolt of lightning. Something inside me was drawn to her. There was something in here eyes that was alluring and mysterious at the same time. I was hungry to know more about her. She fascinated me with a curiosity I couldn't let go.

As the dinner was starting to wind down, I asked them both out on dates for the next day. How could I not when they were both at the same table with me? I set up a date for Anna-Blond for 1:00 and Anna-Red for 4:00 the next day. Anna-Red needed to take a taxi to get home. I paid for dinner and gave her enough money for her taxi ride home. Anna-Blond was going to walk home so I asked if I could walk with her.

As we walked I asked her if Anna-Red was a friend of hers. She said no, that they had just met that night, but that they seemed to really hit it off and hoped to remain friends. It was a cold night in the mid 30's. I asked if I could hold her hand. I said I would not normally ask such a thing after a first date, but I am only here for five more days it changes some things from the norm. She said, "My hands are warm in my pocket." I told her my hands would keep hers warm. She agreed and we held hands for another kilometer as we walked to her house. No, there was no good night kiss. That would not be appropriate. She called a taxi for me and I told her I looked forward to seeing her the next day. She told me she would be more comfortable if I had a translator there. So the next morning I made the arrangements.

At this point, I was still just enjoying the experience and I did not see my Anna-Blond as "the one" – at least not yet.

Several years later we were able to meet up with Anna-Red and her husband in Phoenix. We remain connected to this day.

As a footnote, Anna-Red met a man from the US about a year later and they live in Arizona today. My Anna and Anna-Red stayed connected and we had a fantastic time meeting up with them a short while after she arrived in the US.

MY SECOND DATE WITH ANNA-BLOND

Anna spoke very broken English – enough for rough communication, but she wanted to be able to fully communicate all of her thoughts without having to fight to find the words or use a dictionary. So, I started off that morning by hiring a translator for my date through the romance tour company. I told them about my 1:00 o'clock and 4:00 o'clock dates and gave them the names and cell phone numbers for both girls. It was all set up in less than five minutes and I went off to enjoy a leisurely morning of walking the streets of Nikolaev, Ukraine! What a life. I wondered what the guys back home were doing!

12:30 rolled around and I started asking about the arrangements. I was told that the translator would meet me in the hotel lobby at 12:45. I went to the lobby and waited. At 12:45 a middle aged woman walked in and asked for Mark. I was surprised since most of the other translators had been younger women. But I reasoned that I was not there to date the translator so I greeted her cheerfully. She introduced herself as Vera.

We went to the curb to wait for the taxi. By the time we got in the taxi it was already 1:00 o'clock so I gave her

Anna's number so she could call her to let her know we were on our way. Anna was already at the street curb in front of her house waiting and asked the translator, "Where is my boy?" It was very cute that I was already her boy after one date the night before.

As we drove up to the corner where I'd said goodnight to her the night before, I was able to see her full visage in daylight and I have to admit – she took my breath away. I had not captured her full image before. She looked radiant in her high heel boots and long black coat. Her blond hair was long and full – flowing down to her belt line. She had a lady-like posture and grace about her that was noble and elegant.

We drove to a local restaurant that had a wonderful atmosphere; a steakhouse. It was adorned in stone work walls with tapestries. A fish tank was made part of one wall. Smooth jazz music played in the background.

Working with Vera was effortless and it was like she was part of the dialog. And yet, at the same time, it was as if the two of us were alone. I don't even remember all that was said that first hour of our date, but I knew she was the one. It struck me in a profound way. I had been so specific about what I was looking for, how we would interact, and how I would feel in her presence. Now, to be with her, it was like déjà vu. This was the one. I was done. I just didn't know what to do next.

I told Vera quietly to the side that I thought Anna was the one for me. I didn't know what to do now. She was

118

delighted. The matchmaker in her came out. She smiled, patted me on the knee and quietly said, "I will help you."

Vera was translator, guide, and friend.

The three of us feasted on delightful conversation for another two hours. Once Anna understood that I was interested in her exclusively, we set up more dates together – including dinner later that night. We came back to the same restaurant and ended the evening on the dance floor in the back room where we slow danced together – just the two of us. We gazed deeply in each other's eyes for minutes on end, and then held each other again as we slowly moved in rhythm.

MORE DATING TO DO

Even though I had met the girl I thought I had come for, she was not available again until the next night. I still had one date I set up for myself in the next town with a lady I had written to, Tatyana.

Here's an important thought you should keep in mind: Even though you may think you have found the one, don't close off your options yet. Get good feedback from your translator and your coaches. I've seen way too many men cancel all of the dates they'd set up just to wish they could re-set them again.

I went with the romance tour to the next city to have my date with Tatyana – then I would catch a taxi back to keep my date with Anna that night when she got off work. Tatyana didn't want to go to the social, so she met me outside where she had a taxi waiting. She selected a taxi driver who owned a Rolls Royce. I hadn't seen such a beautiful car in the entire country until that point. She took me to a very upscale Japanese Sushi restaurant that could have been a hot spot in San Francisco or New York.

She had already arranged for a translator, who was a delightful woman in her mid 20's. The evening was magical. In all honesty, if I hadn't already met Anna, I would have had no hesitation in pursuing Tatyana – and we would have made for a great couple. That is the power in having options. Go with your heart, but don't leave the country without at least one or more girls you wish to follow up with. It may be in future correspondence with girls you dated that one rises to the top if one didn't while you were there.

In that one-hour taxi ride back to Nikolaev for my date with Anna that night, I had mixed feelings. Tatyana was funny, comfortable to be with, and was genuinely in to me. But once I saw my Anna again the confusion vanished: my heart confirmed that she was the one for me.

Lyudmila, age 22

CHAPTER NINE

I THINK I'VE FOUND HER!
NOW WHAT?

If you do find one wonderful woman you want to pursue while you are still in her country; your first thought will be to spend as much time with her as you can while you are there. If I'd been on a Quest Tour it wouldn't be a problem because I'd be in the same city all week anyway. But now that I'd met Anna and felt that she was the one for me, I had to ditch the romance tour company, make my own hotel reservations, and plan to stay the week in Nikolaev to solidify this new relationship as best I could.

But in doing so, I also started to feel a lot of pressure come over me. What do I do now? How is she feeling about all of this? Think about it. She just signed up with a dating service a few days before. Yes, she's had a wonderful time with you, but in the back of her mind she also knows that you are leaving in a few days. Is she wondering how much she means to you? What will happen when you return? Will you forget her?

Your mind starts to scramble. What can you accomplish in a few days? "Maybe I should propose marriage now," you ponder. "Maybe I should tell her I love her. But what if she says no or doesn't say she loves me too?"

STOP!

Take a deep breath.

No one is suggesting you propose marriage in the first week you meet. A person who genuinely values the meaning of, "I love you" may not say those words after only knowing someone for one week.

That's when I hear it. That voice of calm comes to me speaking words of wisdom, "Enjoy the small moments. Create memories. Smell the sweet fragrance of romance's intoxicating perfume. She's not going anywhere. And you are not going to be removed from her life just because you leave for home. So relax and build some fun memories while you deepen the connection." Bingo. I'm good again.

BECOMING BOYFRIEND AND GIRLFRIEND

Before I would leave the country in five days; I wanted to know that we were committed to each other to some extent. When I got back to my room I called Vera and asked her what she thought I should do. She said the reasonable thing would be to ask her to be my girlfriend – sort of like binding us to an exclusive relationship so we can get to know each other better. She also suggested that I get her a promise ring to help close the deal. So Vera met up with me and we went shopping.

That sneaky matchmaker had already gotten Anna to disclose her ring size! We went from store to store until I found one that I thought was perfect – and Vera agreed. The store put the ring in a heart-shaped red velvet box and I brought it with me to dinner that night – back at the steakhouse once again.

When the moment was right, I told Anna that I was so glad we met and that I was impressed with the wonderful person she is. I told her that it was my intention to get to know her more – even after I went back to my home. I wanted to ask her if she would agree to be my girlfriend, so that we would take a few months to just date and write to each other exclusively (we didn't have Skype or Viber back in 2006 that I was aware of).

"You can always put yourself back on the network of active profiles if it doesn't work out between us," I told her. "If you would agree to be my girlfriend I would like for you to wear this ring."

With that said, I opened the box in front of her to reveal this gold ring that had an ornate infinity circle design with a small gem set in the middle. She gasped for a moment. The lighting was just right to make it shine.

This is that critical moment when you've asked for a decision . . . now, just shut up and wait for the response.

But she hesitated. She said something to Vera in Russian. Vera explained to me, "You are the first international man she has ever met. She really likes you and doesn't want to lose you, but she has nothing to compare you to."

I did the man thing at that moment. I closed the lid and put the box back in my coat pocket. "That is not a problem," I said. "I don't want to be the one to choose her until she feels that she wants to choose me as well."

There was stunned silence. The two of them looked at each other. They spoke in Russian for a few minutes back and forth as I waited quietly for her response.

Finally, Vera leaned over to me and asked, "Would you please put that ring back on the table?" So I did as she asked. I opened the box again and they both let out an audible sigh.

Vera leaned over to me again and said, "Would you please put that ring on her finger?" Anna held out her hand toward me and I placed the ring on her finger. Vera fought to hold back the tears.

The moment I placed the promise ring on her finger was as magical as you can imagine.

Let me stop here long enough to say two things. First, boyfriend/girlfriend is about as much of a commitment as anyone should expect to get out of such a short time. But, if you were on a second or third date, it would be good for you to know for certain where you stand. You need to be able to make the most of your time. If she's not feeling what you are feeling, you need to know. By the third date you should put out some kind of feeler to see if you are on the same page.

I recommend you ask what I call, "The Three Qualifying Questions". You'll learn about these more in the "Closing the Deal" training video that you receive when you sign up for a Quest Tour, but here's the essence of it.

You make three statements and then ask her the three corresponding questions:

1. I want to let you know that I came here with a serious interest in finding my half

2. I have truly enjoyed spending time with you

3. You are exactly the type of woman I was hoping to meet

Then you ask her:

1. Did you come to the event with a serious interest in trying to find your half?

2. Have you been enjoying the time with me?

3. Am I the type of man you would hope to meet as a potential match?

If she's not serious then you will know before you're all the way back home. You should still have time to connect again with the other women who sparked your interest in the Meet & Match Events.

If you were the one who's not certain, it would probably be a more realistic goal to just create a strong bond and wonderful memories and then continue the connection once you have returned home.

She will miss you like crazy. Once she has begun her work-a-day life again she'll remember the incredible time she had with you – and you may as well. While you are reflecting on your time, your heart may be longing for her – and that is when you call to propose the boyfriend/girlfriend relationship. Next time your trip will be entirely about her.

MEETING THE FAMILY

Vera was from an older generation where the head of the family had to approve all relationships. So, from Vera's perspective, meeting the family had to be the next step. She had this whole process planned out in her mind. She wanted to set up a meeting where all of the relatives would gather to meet me. There would be food and drink. It would be a big deal in the family. I needed to bring gifts – and wear a suit.

Well, that may have been true for Vera, but it was not the case with Anna. Anna jumped right in and said, "I will decide if this relationship is best for me not my parents. You don't need to meet my family. That may happen when it makes sense."

Every girl will be different in this regard. But the path to meeting the family is definitely something that must be guided by your lady. Let her decide when to meet them and whom you should meet. Don't be concerned that you need someone's blessing unless your girl says it is important.

A good friend of mine has a wonderful girl in his life. At first her family was concerned about their relationship.

The stated concern was that the age gap was too much. He sent a few boxes of gifts to the family. He sent leather goods, salami, cheese and crackers and the like. Suddenly, the family had no problem with him or the age gap!

Your girl will help guide the path with her family. Listen to her.

DATING YOUR GIRL

Once you have picked one to focus on – the one you want to call 'your girl' – the dating changes slightly. One of the ways it changes is just in the time you make for it. Presuming you are on your first trip, you will both work to spend every waking moment together. Most likely you will have to work around her schedule. She may have a job or university classes that she can't get out of – but, trust me, she will try to get out of them.

If you remember, we met on a Sunday, dated on Monday, Tuesday I was in Kherson and Wednesday she got the day off from work. She called Vera and told her to get a taxi to pick me up at 10:00 o'clock in the morning. It was a radiant joy to see her again. The three of us drove along to another neighborhood where we picked up her four year old goddaughter, Nastya. The light bulb in my head went on: she wants to see how I am with kids! This was a test – and a very good sign! She is serious about me.

We spent the day at the zoo and a place called Kid's Planet, similar to Chuck E. Cheese. Since I've had four kids, this was the best test I could have asked for. I had a blast – and won my girl's heart.

Anna wanted to see if I was good with kids. Good with kids? I still am a kid!

On other dates we drove to beaches, national landmarks, museums, and did some shopping. Once she is your girl and you have more time, you can even take her to other cities for your private mini-vacation with her.

The rest is up to your imagination – but let your girl help select the locations since it is her country – and it is good for her to feel like she can help you in some way.

WHEN DO I POP THE QUESTION?

Wow, is that the $64,000 question. Everyone is different, but I can offer some guidelines – and a secret strategy.

This entire strategy for international dating is designed to cut through the dating process to get to the bottom line as quickly as possible. You meet with serious women who are there to find husbands. You are there to find a gorgeous woman who will love you every day of your life. In nine days you accomplish more than you could in two years of dating in your country – and with superior results.

But it can feel like it goes too fast – especially for your girl.

These women are typically very savvy and completely authentic. You can talk about anything – just don't lie to them. You may be able to talk with them about the possibility of married life together – or you may have to go with your gut and just pop the question when your gut tells you the timing is right.

In our case, we had talked about life and the possibilities of marriage. It was very comfortable to do so. In our case we both agreed that neither of us would know for certain if we were right for marriage until she was able to be in my home for at least a few weeks. She needed to see for herself that what I was telling her about my life was true and see if there were any unknown aspects that could

132

make life unbearable. That is completely understandable. I also wanted to see how she would handle life with me before making the relationship legally official. But how to get her to my home so we could both feel certainty was the question. Most women are not this conservative and most of our married couples had become engaged while she was still living in her home country.

So, the question of the hour was, "How can we get her to my home?"

If you do not live in the United States, this process could be as simple as getting her a passport and having her over for a few months. Wow, do I wish it were that simple for US citizens. But, on the other hand, you need to understand that the K-1 Fiancé Visa process has also weeded out the illegal "Russian Bride" scams that had been more prevalent in the past.

We both knew that we could always back out at any point before the "I do's". If you think I am taking this lightly, I am not. I am a big believer in committed marriage. But most adults don't have to go through as much as you will to get to the altar. You might as well get the process going and work through your relationship as you go. In truth, I wonder if the foreign marriages are stronger because of the work they have to go through more work and time to be together!

For us, the K-1 Fiancé Visa process would take at least six months to get through before I had her in my home. That also gave us time to get to know each other better.

Yes, the Fiancé Visa program is a preparation program for married life in America. Yes, you both have to sign affidavits swearing to your intention to marry within 90-days from when she arrives on US soil. But it takes long enough to get through the process that it will also help solidify the relationship – so you'll be completely confident in your decision. And no one is going to put a gun to your head and make you get married if you see that it isn't working out.

The secret strategy is that you can both commit to the K 1 visa process like an engagement period – even though you may not be ready to say absolutely yes to marriage at the time you start the process.

None of that may sound like a very romantic way to "pop the question". Your time for a romantic proposal may come later. But the truth is that you are going to have to work through a lot of paperwork first. By the time you've finished the visa paperwork, you will have spent months more creating a bond that is not questionable. For her the thought of leaving family and country and making a life with you may be less eventful than it could be otherwise if you had to force the issue too soon after meeting.

I am a romantic guy and I was determined to make my marriage proposal a very romantic event. Once she got here and we'd spent three weeks together, I planned a dinner cruise around the San Francisco Bay and Golden Gate Bridge. We had already picked out rings in Ukraine so she could show them to her family, but she did not see them again until I got on one knee and proposed marriage officially to her on that romantic cruise.

Most guys will propose actual marriage in the girl's home country, but this is where you have to follow your heart. I have faith in you. You'll come up with your own way to be romantic with your beauty queen.

I decided to also include my son, Christopher, in the marriage proposal. We both got on one knee. I asked if she'd be my wife and he asked if she'd be his step-mom.

Ryan and Yulia met on a Quest Tour in Ukraine and were married in August of 2014.

CHAPTER 10

GETTING OVER THE GOAL LINE

What is the goal? The goal is to have this incredible beauty in your arms and waking up with her each morning. But you have to walk a path to get there. The biggest obstacle for US citizens is the immigration and visa process. Once that is done, the rest is romance and wedding planning. Let's look at what it is going to take to get from "she's the one" to "she's in your home".

If you are not a US citizen, read this section to get an idea of how immigration processes work. Yours may be similar or simpler. But at least you'll have an idea of what it takes to prove your love and bring home your prize.

What's involved in the U.S. visa process? Many documents to fill out and an endless number of procedures that must be followed . . . but all basically come down to demonstrating these objectives for Homeland Security:

1. Proof that you are a citizen

2. Proof that you have a relationship with her that has included time spent in her country

3. Proof that you can financially support her;

4.   Proof that she is a citizen of the country she claims to be from;

5.   Proof that she has no criminal record;

6.   Proof that she is not carrying any disease into the country.

First, you will submit your application to an immigration office in the US. Once your application for her is approved, it then goes to the US Embassy in her country where she must bring her documents and be interviewed in person. If she is approved, she will be given a fiancé visa stamp in her passport. She must start travel to the US within six months and be married to you within 90 days after arriving or she must go back.

In my case, I met Anna on December 10th and we were married on October 13th of the following year. Ten months from first introductions to "I Do" is a very reasonable timeframe. I had no reason to complain. For me, it was the time I needed to get to know my future wife. By the time I was ready to go get her I was confident that we were right for each other.

Once you have your wedding certificate, you must present it, along with other documents such as a request for change of residence status, to the immigration office before the 90-days are completed.

HIRE A VISA ATTORNEY

I don't even know why anyone would want to navigate the immigration legal waters without an attorney – especially when the rates are so reasonable. Most will even have people on staff who can work with your girl in her language. If you are good at paperwork you may consider those fees to be a waste of money. My personal advice would be to just go with an immigration attorney and make your life easier – but that's totally up to you.

KNOW THIS UP FRONT: On your application you will have to demonstrate that you have spent time with your girl in her country. What they will ask for are things like receipts for travel, dining, lodging, and gifts. One of the requirements at the time I went through this was to have 10 photographs of the two of you together in her country. I tell you this because I know that many people are not big picture takers. Or, if they do take pictures, they don't want to be in the pictures – they just want pictures of their girl. Just have someone take at least 15 pictures of the two of you together in her country. And, be sure to save your airline and hotel receipts.

Finally, be the man and be sure to cover any out of pocket costs she may have on her end to get birth certificates translated, etc.

SET UP WAYS TO COMMUNICATE

This may sound simple, but it is often difficult. One of your top priorities has to be keeping the momentum going and the romantic flame burning. You have created such chemistry and energy between you two and the only way to maintain that momentum is to be in regular communication.

If you both have e-mail addresses and smart phones and speak English – you are so fortunate. Be sure to send text or Viber messages during the day and when you both go to bed at night. Call each other when it makes sense, but be sensitive to her work and class schedules.

You may have to buy a smart phone for her and purchase some minutes and data for her.

After my first trip to Ukraine, when I met my wife-to-be, I probably had the most difficult communication situation you could imagine. Her cell phone did not work with international text messaging – which I did not learn until I returned home. It also would not hold calls very well, which really didn't matter since she was still not comfortable enough with her English to have direct conversations with me. She also had no computer or email address. Now what?

Fortunately, we had Vera – and you can continue to use your translator from your Quest Tour at a very reasonable rate as well. One solution could have been for me to send an email to Vera. Then have Vera call Anna and read it to her in Russian. Anna could then tell her what

140

to say in response and I could get an email back from Vera with the message. The process would probably take two or three days from start to finish, but it would work. That is close to what I ended up doing, but I made it one step more personal.

I had a personal website that I put up with Microsoft FrontPage (do you remember that program from 1998?). There was an option to create a bulletin board. I would send Vera an email with what I wanted to say and asked her to send it back to me in Russian. Then I would post the Russian message for Anna to read. She would go to an Internet café to rent a computer and pull up the bulletin board. She could then read my message in Russian and reply to it in Russian. I would look for her messages and then copy and paste them into an email I would send to Vera. Vera would email me Anna's message to me in English and the process would continue.

We kept on this way for two months until I flew out to visit her again. On that trip her English had improved enough that we were able to fully communicate with each other without Vera translating. I also bought her a top of the line cell phone and had it unlocked so she could use it in Ukraine.

When I got home after that trip, we talked on the phone every few days and sent text messages to each other every day. The bulletin board was only used for me to send her photos. Facebook would be the option I'd use today.

That was a lot of freakin' work and I could have saved a lot of time and money by just keeping up our letter writing through the agency. The cost will be defined. They can handle the translation. They can deliver photos back and forth. Why didn't I think of that before? I don't know. Maybe it's a guy thing. We want to fix stuff ourselves and not ask for directions. Who knows?

Don't be discouraged. There are always solutions. Just keep in mind that you have to keep up your momentum for six to eight months until you can be together forever.

THINGS SHE WILL NEED TO DO AS WELL

She will work with your immigration attorney's staff to complete the documents she needs for her application. You may also want to help her start taking English classes.

Finally, you may also want to help her get some driving lessons and a driver's license from her country. Check with your state, but California accepts valid out of state and country drivers' licenses for temporary uses. Once she gets to your home, you do want to help her to be able to get around on her own and not feel trapped.

GET BACK TO HER

Back to the subject of keeping the momentum going; you should plan on visiting your girl within 60 to 90 days after your first trip if at all possible with your work schedule. Going on your own can be very reasonable. When I went to see Anna in February after meeting her in December, I searched the Internet for discount travel and found some incredible deals. Lodging can be very reasonable if you let your girl set it up. They tend to hike the hotel prices for Americans in many cases. Keep checking those discount airline ticket websites for the best deals.

On a subsequent trip we took a taxi to a historical site overlooking the Black Sea

TRY NOT TO EXPLODE

At first glance you might think I mean that from a negative perspective. Quite the contrary. She is going to make you want to be with her more and more every day. The way she loves you and talks with you makes you want to hold her and be with her. You can't help but look at her photos every day – especially her profile photos and the ones of you together.

These will feel like the longest six to eight months of your life; but don't go crazy. Just enjoy the anticipation. Someday this will just be a period of time you look back at as part of your courtship.

SOMETHING SPECIAL

On my third trip I gave Anna a small digital camera with a 2GB memory card (before iPhones). My intention was that I thought she might want to take photos of her friend and hometown to remember after she leaves.

However, when I saw her on my next visit, she gave me the disc and asked me to bring it up on my computer for viewing. She had connected with a friend of hers and shot dozens of bikini pictures of her at the beach, laying on the rocks, etc. They know how to make you happy and it makes them happy to know they impact your life positively. They want to give you things to make you think of them. She wants to know that she is on your mind – all the time.

After giving Anna a digital camera she decided to create pictures that would keep her on my mind. Oh, yeah. She's mine.

GO GET HER - SHE'S YOURS

Finally, when you have completed the legal process and she has the Fiancé Visa stamp in her passport, I recommend that you get on a plane and escort her home. Chances are she has not traveled much in her life. As bright and capable as she is, it is a much nicer touch – and more romantic – if you can go get her and share the ride home. It will be one of the most enjoyable trips you ever take.

David met Katya on a Quest Tour in January of 2014 and were married in her hometown of Nikolaev, Ukraine, eight months later.

CHAPTER ELEVEN

THE 90-DAY FIANCE

You did it. You're off the plane and in your home with your beauty queen. You will be exhausted and want to take a few days just to recover.

Then what? You have four objectives:

1. Get her connected to her family at home

2. Get her connected with your life and world

3. Make the engagement, wedding planning, and wedding ceremony about her

4. Complete the legal work

I call these the '90-days of love' because you will make this time all about her – with most of the work on your end. She is the one making all of the adjustments. She is the one getting ready to be married without her family. She is the one experiencing culture shock. She is a bright girl. She will let you know if you are moving too quickly. But, in the same way you didn't know what to do when you were in her country; she won't know what to do in yours.

CULTURE SHOCK

Culture shock may be different for each girl. Some are overwhelmed by massive retail and commercialism. Others will be shocked that there are so many fat people. Still others are appalled by the lack of concern for good fashion or common courtesies.

Foreign girls are also usually unprepared for what they feel are people who are too friendly and fake with their happy greetings. My wife even questioned Walmart greeters, "Why do they want to know how I'm doing? They don't know me?" And, the open acceptance of gay lifestyles may be offensive to them.

It may be difficult for her to find food that is nutritious or similar to her liking. Don't just make her eat the fatty junk food that is all around us. Help her find places for healthy food. If she is from Asia, Latin America, or the Russian-speaking countries, see if there are local restaurants that serve what she is accustomed to.

She may think that things are too perfect, the streets too clean, and life is too easy.

DON'T MAKE THE MISTAKE OF POINTING OUT TO HER HOW LIFE IN YOUR COUNTRY IS BETTER THAN HERS

She may initially think that her home country is better and our way of living is sloppy, fat, and narcissistic. Just listen to her and acknowledge when she has a valid point. If she is willing to love you through richer or poorer, she will learn to love you wherever you live. Just don't make your differences a source of conflict. Learn to love her unique perspective and blend yours with hers. Remember, you didn't travel around the world to find an American girl. You don't want to force her to conform.

In time, she will learn to love it here with you. Some of them won't realize how they have come to love life with you until a year or two later when they go back home to visit family and have that real-time comparison in front of them. You just can't make her come to the conclusion that America is better. She will come to her own conclusions in her own time.

GETTING HER CONNECTED WITH HER FAMILY

One of the things you will want to do right away is get her a smart phone with a discount calling plan to her home country. You want her to be able to call home. That is where she'll share her excitement about her new life – with family who speak her language. They'll usually be excited for her, as well. After my wife had been with me for nearly a year we finally got her mother a computer, Internet access, and a Skype account. Now their communication is free of any costs and they get to talk eye to eye with video. You've got to love technology when it works!

GETTING TO SEE YOUR WORLD

Take some time during that first month to take short trips. Show her some places of interest around you. It could be a hike in the mountains, trip to the beach, or even a day in Disneyland.

Introduce her to the wonderful things in your own part of the world.

Most importantly, help her find out where the resources are. Where is the grocery store and closest Wal-Mart or Costco? It's interesting to me how many of these ladies love the discount shopping places. Perhaps it gives them a sense that they are helping the family save money – or just the fun of shopping where everything is under one roof.

Finally, on the subject of getting around your world, help her learn to drive in your area and get a driver's license for her.

MEETING FRIENDS AND FAMILY

Friendships and family are important to everyone. You can't make her become friends with someone, but she will respect people you consider to be your friends. Prepare your friends and family to welcome her. If you know of good people in your community who are from her country you might help he make that connection. Just keep in mind that not everyone from her homeland will be a good person for her to connect with.

If she can find a girlfriend to take walks or go shopping, that will go a long way for both of you.

WEDDING PLANNING

Hopefully she has connected with another woman in your world who can help her with wedding planning. You should allow her to have some joy in picking out a dress and helping put together her own wedding. Even though time is short, you can still put together a decent wedding. I went directly to an event rental business to get tables, chairs, linens, and an arbor. They also introduced me to a good florist. We had 32 close friends and family and enjoyed a wonderful day. But most important, my wife was gorgeous and had the wedding she wanted.

Some have even less time and end up with a Justice of the Peace ceremony or Las Vegas-style wedding. Whatever you end up doing, just be sure to include your bride in the planning. Finally, make sure you take some good photos that she can send home to her family.

FINISHING THE PAPERWORK

Set the date for your wedding to be at least two to three weeks prior to your 90-day deadline. Even when you have the certified wedding certificate in your hands, you are not done. It must be submitted with more documents. This is where you petition to change her status to permanent resident, ask for travel documents, and a work permit.

In case you are not familiar with the Green Card system, let me explain. In short, your permanent status prior to citizenship is given by the issuing of a Green Card. The first issuance is for two years. At the end of two years you must re-appear at an INS office to show that you're still married and the prospects of a continued relationship are good. She will then be issued a Permanent Residence that's good for 10 years. She can apply for US citizenship as soon as she has this permanent residence card.

I can tell you this, once you're done with the paperwork, you'll both breathe a giant sigh of relief.

Finally, it's time for Happily Ever After!

A New Life with New Adventures

It's the Beginning of Happily Ever After

CHAPTER TWELVE

HAPPILY EVER AFTER

CREATING THE LIFE OF YOUR DREAMS

You left your castle determined to find the perfect queen to complete your kingdom. You traveled the world and spent time with many beautiful women – any of them would love to be chosen by such a king. They put on their best to impress you. You created such stories of adventure that you knew would capture the imaginations of your kindred back home who eagerly awaited word from your travels.

Then you met the woman of intrigue who captured your attention. She is graceful, feminine, sensuous, and captivating. It did not take long to declare that you wanted to know her better. Your romance was like none other. You brought flowers and took her on wonderful dates. She treasures the small gifts you gave to her to this very day.

But to bring her back to your country would be a task for the bold. You negotiated with governments to arrange for her transport. As you waited, you continued to write and speak with her and send her gifts and expressions from your heart. You gave gifts to her family and they were glad for their daughter to have such an opportunity; the chance at living a life as the wife of a nobleman; such as yourself.

The day finally arrives when you can bring her home. The greatest travel you have ever experienced was that first trip with her at your side.

You took the time to make her feel relaxed and welcomed in your castle. You took her on short visits to see the region surrounding your kingdom and created new experiences and memories for her.

Now she is your bride . . . your queen . . . your lover . . . your wife. She is part of you and will bring grace and love to the walls of your castle. In as much as you had desired to rescue the beauty, she, in turn, rescued you.

The circle is complete and now you get to live your *Happily Ever After.*

WHAT DOES HAPPILY EVER AFTER LOOK LIKE?

What else will you do now? Well, that is up to the two of you to imagine and create. What has she always dreamed her life would be like? Believe it or not, my wife negotiated that she'd get a puppy and a kitten on that first date with Vera. Within a year after her arriving here we had two dogs and a cat. Your wife will want to create a sense of family and identity with you – even if it is just a family of two.

The topic of work and career may change as she gets settled in. Let it be a fluid aspect of your new life together. Just figure it out as you go. One man married a woman who had been a doctor in Russia. When she came here, she did what was required so she could practice medicine here. Today, she is a doctor at a major hospital. Many of them have university degrees from their home countries that will transfer.

Sometimes the women are adamant that they need to wait to come home with you until after they finish a certain semester of their schooling. You may have to do some compromising, but don't get on her case later if she delayed coming for a degree she didn't end up using. Her instincts

157

may be to get the degree in case you leave her and she has to fend for herself. Once she feels secure in your love she may not feel so pressured to have to do anything with that education. Just love her. You may still be too good to be true in her mind. I'm serious.

I hope you will create a *new* vision of your perfect life, the way you did in Chapter 3. But this time, you get to do it with her. Let her dream with you about the life you want to create together. There is nothing to stop you. Make both of your dreams come true. Be the golden man – her king and she will strive to be the woman of your dreams as well.

WHEW!

What an adventure! You traveled the world in search of amazing beauty and found a love most men only dream about.

Was all of this worth it? Just look in her eyes and you tell me! But beyond that, what is your alternative? You could live alone. You could marry an American girl and hope your odds are better than most. No, you made a different choice.

Was it worth it? You walk down the street and see the envy of men who wish they had what you have – but what you have is more than a beauty by your side. Even more beautiful is the way you interact with each other. It is delightful and richly satisfying in every respect.

Many men don't believe they could really have such beauty and love as a part of their daily life. Their lack of belief is exactly why they don't.

Other men have told me that they wish they had what I have. I tell them that they can have it and where to find it; but will they go get it? It is available to those who take action and just go after it. The system is in place to give expert assistance at every stage. Why wouldn't you go see for yourself instead of remaining curious forever – wondering what might have been?

It is sad to think about the other women who are still back in Ukraine hoping their Happily Ever After. There are so many good women and I hope to use this book to spark a movement so more men will go and discover this match made in heaven: good men finding good women.

If you do what I have suggested in this book, you will become very clear about what you want – and now you know where to find it. In like fashion, my wife told me that she knew I would be her husband the first night we met. She tells me, "All of my dreams are coming into reality just as I imagined they would." She was also clear about what she was looking for.

Right now someone out there is imagining a life with you and you don't even know it.

After spending just a short time with Anna, I knew she was the one for me. I had the clarity and confidence in my decision to pursue her. Yet it still astonishes me that I was able to write this first letter to her before I left – after having just met her that same week. Every word has proven true:

My Darling Anna:

It is 3:00 in the morning and I cannot sleep. My mind is full of thoughts of you.

Soon I will be in California at least in body. But my mind and heart will remain with you.

I have lived enough years to have known many people in different parts of this world. I have never met one as wonderful as you. You are a giving person, loving toward children and animals, and not afraid of hard work. You are also stubborn, strong in your values, and a fighter. At the same time, you are still the child who loves to play, as I am.

Your laughter is as refreshing as the warm glow of the sun. Your smile is like a masterpiece of art - there is nothing like it. Your eyes write books and tell stories in the simplest of glances - they are limitless in beauty and in expression. Your eyes whisper and tell me that there is a woman of mystery hiding in wait - longing to be discovered by the one with the key - and so I search for the key to your heart.

I am a king with a growing kingdom. I have earned the respect of important men. But you are the one who has captured the king's heart.

I am proud that you wear my ring. Part of my identity is now connected with you - it may just be for a season of life - or it may be for all time. God will make it known to both of us and we will be glad for the time we are given, however long or short.

I learn more of you with each moment we share together. Each time I see something new I did not see before. Should we share moments together for the rest of our lives - I know I would still be discovering new insights into your soul - it is deep and limitless.

I am grateful to God that he did not let me find the person I came to see in Nikolaev. He had another plan. I think he takes great pleasure in such surprises.

I believe that our lives will be joined together forever - but only God knows for certain.

Have a wonderful day, my love.

With love from my heart,

Your Mark

Together you will build a relationship that is unique to you and your lady. It can give you both a lifetime of meaningful love and deep satisfaction. You will become a better man for having taken the journey. You will understand other cultures and ways people experience daily life. You will bring some of that home with you so you can take the best of both worlds and make a family that is special to you. I wish all men would have such an experience and understanding of the world.

As I finish writing the last words of this book, I have to recount to you my evening last night. Anna and I were snuggling on the couch watching a movie with the dogs at our sides. When the movie was over, she glanced over at me and reached up to touch my cheek. I asked, "What?" She simply replied, "I am so happy I married you. I am the happiest woman in the world."

And with that, I conclude the book as I began – with a beautiful woman reclining on my chest. This has been my daily life for quite some time now. I am deeply loved by one of the most beautiful women in the world – and, in return, I make her feel deeply loved as well.

Now you know the secret – and she has thousands of sisters out there just hoping to someday meet you.

ONE PARTING REQUEST . . .

I would just ask for your help in spreading the word.

Share this secret. Let other men know that there is hope. And in doing so, you provide hope to the most wonderful women in the world as well. Hope that someday they may see their king walk into a ballroom and pursue them to win their heart.

Let me know about your journey as you go. Go to our website: http://www.DreamConnections.com and join our list. You can email me a question at Mark@DreamConnections.com. We're here for you and want to share in your experience.

May God bless you and guide you as you go on your quest to find your queen.

And above all, follow your heart,

Mark

Mark Edward Davis

"I am so blessed to be able to do what I love and with the people I love."

Mark Edward Davis has been a men's coach for more than 20 years. He conducted his first time-management course at age 25. But his greatest career legacy has been the creation of Dream Connections' Quest Tour system along with his wife, Anna. They have helped form many new marriages and families and proven that their relationship strategies work.

They have appeared on The TODAY Show with Matt Lauer, the Dr. Phil Show, the Women's Entertainment Network (WeTV), Discovery Channel's TLC UK, plus more than 50 radio interviews.

Mark & Anna Davis also founded Abundance Int'l – a non-profit that supports the orphans in Ukraine.

He and his wife, Anna, and son, Christopher, live in North Las Vegas, Nevada. Mark's three adult children and three grandchildren live in California.

Our Story

Anna - Growing Up in Ukraine

Mark – His Life Before Anna

When Mark Met Anna in 2006

Dating Anna in Ukraine 2007

Mark & Anna Married October 2007

Anna Tries Modeling in the US

Beginnings of Dream Connections

Quest Tours Move to Nikolaev

Christmas Reunion at Disneyland

Our Work with the Orphanage

Many Happily Ever After Stories

We Feel Truly Blessed – Join Us!

Mark

www.DreamConnections.com

Dedicated to
your
Happily Ever
After

INDEX

1. Website for the Miss Universe Pageant:
   http://www.missuniverse.com

2. IMBRA:
   http://www.govtrack.us/congress/billtext.xpd?bill=h10
   9-3657

3. Immigration Report:
   http://dreamconnections.com/immigration-report/

4. CIA World Stats:
   https://www.cia.gov/library/publications/the-world
   factbook/index.html

5. MSN article "Are Boys and Endangered Species?"
   http://health.msn.com/pregnancy/articlepage.aspx?cp-
   documentid=100171768

6. Bly, Robert, Iron John, A Book About Men
      DaCapo Press, Eleven Cambridge Center,
   Cambridge, MA 02142. 2004

7. Eldredge, John, Wild at Heart, Discovering the Secret of
   a Man's Soul   ThomasNelson, Inc., PO Box 141000,
   Nashville, TN 37214. 2001

8. Eldredge, John & Stasi, Captivating, Unveiling the
   Mystery of a Woman's Soul   Thomas Nelson, Inc.,
   PO Box 141000, Nashville, TN 37214. 2005

Made in the USA
Charleston, SC
15 February 2016